*Anthropologist Kenneth Chapman visited San Ildefonso Pueblo
in the 1930s and talked with potter Maria Martinez.
Chapman asked her when she was born, to which she is said
to have responded, "I am here."*

I AM HERE

TWO THOUSAND YEARS OF SOUTHWEST INDIAN ARTS AND CULTURE

ANDREW HUNTER WHITEFORD

STEWART PECKHAM

RICK DILLINGHAM

NANCY FOX

KATE PECK KENT

LABORATORY OF ANTHROPOLOGY

MUSEUM OF INDIAN ARTS AND CULTURE

MUSEUM OF NEW MEXICO PRESS · PUBLISHERS · SANTA FE

The Laboratory of Anthropology, the Museum of Indian Arts and Culture, and the Museum of New Mexico Press are units of the Museum of New Mexico, a division of the State Office of Cultural Affairs.

This publication was made possible, in part, through the generous contribution of funding from the Museum of New Mexico Foundation.

Cover, ii, vi, viii: Photographs by Edward S. Curtis, from *The North American Indian.*

Museum of New Mexico Press
Series in Southwestern Culture

Library of Congress Cataloging-in-Publication Data

Laboratory of Anthropology (Museum of New Mexico)
  I Am Here.

  (Series in Southwestern culture)
  Bibliography: p.
  Includes index.
  1. Indians of North America—Southwest, New—Art—Catalogs. 2. Indians of North America—Southwest, New—Antiquities—Catalogs. 3. Southwest, New—Antiquities—Catalogs. 4. Laboratory of Anthropology (Museum of New Mexico)—Catalogs. I. Dillingham, Rick. II. Title. III. Series.
  E78.S7L23   1988   745′.08997078   87-22112
  ISBN 0-89013-173-2
  ISBN 0-89013-174-0 (pbk.)

Printed in Japan by Dai Nippon Printing
Typography by Business Graphics, Inc., Albuquerque
Designed by Christopher Beisel and Bonnie Bishop
Production by Daniel Martinez
Photography by Douglas Kahn

MUSEUM of NEW MEXICO PRESS
P.O. Box 2087
Santa Fe, New Mexico 87503

5 4 3 2

The following objects are School of American Research Collections housed in the Museum of New Mexico: Pages 15, 18, 19 (bottom), 70, 77, 85, 96, 99, and Figures 8–10, 18, 20, 21, 25–30, 32, 37, 44, 45, 48, 49, 52–54, 57–60, 65, 66, 68, 70, 72–76, 78, 81–86, 88–91, 93, 97, 98, 102, 104–107, 109, 110, 113–115, 118 (far right), 119, 120, 122, 123, 127–129, 131, 142, 145, 147, 150–152, 155, 164, 167–169, 183 (left). Figure 5 courtesy of Utah Museum of Natural History, University of Utah. Figure 15 courtesy of Arizona State Museum, University of Arizona. Figure 56 loan of Bruce Bernard. Figure 80 loan of Mrs. T. Elmes. Figures 130, 133 loan of Bernard Spitz.

In Memory of Kate Peck Kent
1914–1987

CONTENTS

FOREWORD

BEING ASKED TO WRITE A FOREWORD to the first publication to emanate from the new Museum of Indian Arts and Culture means something very special to me. The completion of the new museum, with its fresh, informative exhibits, is a dream come true. After almost eighty years of growth, the Museum of New Mexico can finally boast of having a fine new museum devoted solely to the cultural heritage of the American Indian populations of New Mexico and the greater Southwest. Among the artifacts in its first exhibits are many old friends, objects that I have handled many times; some, perhaps, that I personally excavated. All are cherished.

I spent thirty-two years of my professional life on the staff of the Museum of New Mexico. When I joined the staff in 1937, the museum and its sister institution, the School of American Research, had already achieved national and some international recognition for their role in the shaping of southwestern anthropology. Dr. Edgar Lee Hewett, founding director of the museum and SAR, was a legendary figure in southwestern scientific circles. Among his many accomplishments was to initiate the first field training programs in ethnology and archaeology in New Mexico. Many of his students and junior colleagues went on to make important contributions to American anthropology, among them Alfred Vincent Kidder, Sylvanus G. Morley, John P. Harrington, Neil Judd, Kenneth M. Chapman, and Jesse Nusbaum.

When Hewett invited me to join his staff, the Museum of New Mexico was housed in two buildings on the plaza in downtown Santa Fe—the Palace of the Governors and the Museum of Fine Arts. Museum administrative offices shared the Palace with the staff of the School of American Research and the Historical Society of New Mexico, while the remainder of the Palace contained exhibits of the prehistoric Southwest. Two of the galleries were devoted entirely to Hewett's excavations at Puyé cliff dwellings and in the Rito de Frijoles (Bandelier National Monument), where Hewett's first archaeological field schools were held.

In 1938 the museum acquired the old armory building adjacent to the Palace, where Bertha Dutton, curator of ethnology, installed exhibits reflecting contemporary Indian life and culture. There was never enough storage space in the early years. Until the 1940s, all of the archaeological materials were stored in the basement of the Museum of Fine Arts. If laboratory analysis or exhibit preparation had to be done, material was hauled across the street to the Palace.

The problem of storage and research space for the anthropology collections was resolved in 1947 when the Laboratory of Anthropology, a Santa Fe research institute started with private funds in 1927, became part of the Museum of New Mexico. But while the Laboratory provided plenty of storage and research space, its two small exhibit galleries were never adequate to exhibit the growing anthropological collections.

I became curator of anthropology exhibits in the 1950s. None of us working in exhibits at the time had any formal training in exhibition design or installation. We had university degrees and were expected to perform field and laboratory research, to lecture and publish on the results of our research, and to design and install meaningful exhibits. Most of my training in exhibits was gained from on-the-job experience, by visiting other museums around the country, by reading, and by trial and error. We had virtually no funds for exhibits in the early years, and the problem of inadequate exhibition space compounded the challenge. We used to visit shops and galleries around the plaza and beg for used display props. What we couldn't beg or borrow we manufactured from scraps acquired from here and there.

In the 1960s and '70s the Museum of New Mexico grew rapidly. The museum began to speak with pride of its new exhibitions unit, an educational department, an office of publications, a newly refurbished Museum of Fine Arts, and a beautiful new exhibition wing for the Museum of International Folk Art. Although I was pleased with the rapid expansion of the museum, I could see that emphasis was slowly being directed away from anthropology and Southwest Indians. By the early 1970s, all Indian cultural exhibits were removed from both the Palace and the Hall of the Modern Indian to make way for history and its collections of artifacts and books. The staff of the Laboratory of Anthropology did the best possible with their small exhibit room, but it had become obvious to many of us that the time had come for the Museum of New Mexico to devote an entire building to its anthropology and Southwest Indian collections.

For most of the 1970s there was much discussion about the need for an Indian museum, about what it should look like, where it should be constructed, and other concerns. Many experts were consulted and innumerable meetings were held. There were those who said an anthropology or Indian cultural unit belonged in the Santa Fe plaza area, and elaborate plans for such a building were drawn and discussed. Finally, though, after several years of debate, the decision was made to build the new museum adjacent to the Laboratory, where its collections were already housed, on a beautiful ridge overlooking the Jemez Mountains and the Valley of the Rio Grande.

After all these years of wishing and hoping to see the birth of an exhibition hall for the American Indian, it is a dream come true to stand in front of the Museum of Indian Arts and Culture, to see what has been accomplished in such a short time, and to realize its promise for the future. With this fine book in hand, and upon passing into the exhibit area for the first time, you are crossing the threshold of a new era which represents the future of the Museum of New Mexico. With such a glorious past, it is exciting to know that the Museum of New Mexico has planned well for its future as it approaches a century of service to all the people of New Mexico.

MARJORIE F. LAMBERT,
Curator Emerita,
Laboratory of Anthropology

PREFACE

THE LABORATORY OF ANTHROPOLOGY opened its doors to the public in September 1931. Its mission was to conduct anthropological research, provide public education, and work to insure the survival and welfare of the native peoples of the Southwest. While pursuing these aims the Laboratory amassed one of the region's finest collections of Indian art and artifacts. In the early years, collection storage areas were open to public viewing. But in 1960, concern for the security of the collections forced the closing of the basement exhibit rooms, leaving only two small ground floor rooms for exhibition of the Laboratory's extensive collection.

In response to a growing public demand for access to the increasing number of artifacts not on display, the 1977 New Mexico Legislature generously appropriated $2.7 million for the design and construction of a Museum of Indian Arts and Culture to serve as an exhibit wing for the Laboratory of Anthropology. Ground was broken for the new museum in October 1984, and the museum opened its doors to the public in July 1987.

The opening of a new museum is an exciting and, at times, daunting process. Not only must bricks and mortar be put in place, but the interior of the building must be furnished with collection storage areas, preparation shops, and all the myriad components of a modern museum facility. Then, exhibition programming and design present the museum staff with one of its most challenging tasks.

From the earliest phases of exhibit design at the Museum of Indian Arts and Culture, there was a consensus among the curatorial staff that an opening exhibit should highlight some of the fine examples of Indian arts and culture in the Laboratory of Anthropology's collections. We wanted not only to exhibit some of the masterpieces of the Laboratory's collections but to relate the story behind the objects. Our goal was to convey some understanding and appreciation of Native American cultural and artistic traditions that extend back more than twelve thousand years in the Southwest.

For an exhibition encompassing so extended a period of culture changes and continuity, we chose to highlight important innovations and achievements, new directions in design and technology, and the impacts of trade and intercultural contact. The result was "Treasures from the Laboratory of Anthropology: Two Thousand Years of Indian Arts and Culture." This book serves as a permanent record of that opening exhibition.

The design of the "Treasures" exhibit began in earnest in the summer of 1986. Our first task was to assemble a team of scholars to draft the exhibit story line and select objects for the exhibition. We were fortunate to enlist the services of some of the Southwest's leading authorities on Indian arts and material culture. Stewart Peckham, Curator Emeritus at the Laboratory of Anthropology and a leading authority on New Mexico prehistory, agreed to curate the prehistoric pottery portion of the exhibit. Rick Dillingham, co-owner of the Mudd-Carr Gallery in Santa Fe and an expert on Pueblo ceramic traditions, volunteered to curate the historic pottery. Dr. Andrew Hunter Whiteford, Professor Emeritus of Anthropology at Beloit College and a leading authority on Native American baskets, curated the basketry portions of the exhibit. The late Kate Peck Kent, formerly Associate Professor Emeritus of Anthropology at Denver University and a leading expert on southwestern textiles, undertook the textile curation chores. Nancy Fox, Senior Curator of Collections at the Laboratory of Anthropology, brought her considerable expertise in southwestern jewelry to the project.

It was decided early in the design process to adhere to a simple cultural-historical story line. Consistent with this approach, the curators divided the exhibit into four discrete time periods bounded by pivotal dates in the evolution of Southwest material culture traditions. The first period, the Prehistoric, would include material from one thousand years before the dawning of the Christian era to the year 1598, when Spanish colonists established the first permanent settlement in New Mexico. The second, or Early Historic Period, would span three centuries, from 1598 to the arrival of the railroad in 1880. The third, or Late Historic Period, would span the late nineteenth and first half of the twentieth centuries, from 1880 to 1960. And the last, or Contemporary Period, would include objects created after 1960.

It was determined that selection of objects for the exhibit would be based on criteria that would emphasize important patterns of change and continuity through time. Thus, the critical problem of selecting some 300 objects from a collection of over 50,000 was partially resolved by defining the scope and content of the story that was being told. "Treasures" were defined as objects that would illustrate evolutionary trends or new directions for old traditions.

For this exhibition the Museum is indebted to the scholarship and dedication of a group of superb curators, but not to them alone. I would like to extend a special thanks to Christopher Beisel, who designed both the exhibition and, with Bonnie Bishop, the book. Christopher's artistic talents and design sensitivities are exceeded only by his patience with curators and conservators. To Juan Alvarez and his staff at the Exhibitions Bureau of the Museum of New Mexico, our thanks for assistance with all the myriad tasks associated with exhibit fabrication and installation. Special thanks to fabricators Thayer Carter and Nick Silva; preparators Phillip Nakamura, J. Pearson, and Janet Persons; and graphic designer Marmika.

The Conservation Bureau of the Museum of New Mexico worked many long hours under a demanding installation schedule to stabilize and conserve objects for the exhibit. Our thanks to Claire Munzenrider, Bettina Raphael, Molly Mahaffey, Landis Smith, and Nora Pickens for their efforts to ensure that priceless objects survived the rigors of handling and public exhibition.

Much of the credit for the quality of this publication goes to Douglas Kahn, who photographed the artifacts. The remaining credit must go to the Publications Department of the Museum of New Mexico, especially its director, Jim Mafchir, and chief editor, Mary Wachs. Special thanks also to Curt Schaafsma, Nancy Fox, Louise Stiver, and Theresa Herrera of the Laboratory of Anthropology, whose efforts in the last few weeks of exhibit installation and toward the publication of *I Am Here* have been invaluable.

Finally, I would like to express my appreciation to Marge Lambert, whose foreword to this book helps place our collective efforts in historical perspective. Marge is one of many visionary scholars who have graced the halls of the Laboratory of Anthropology over the past sixty years. Our most important measure of success on this project is to realize some of the goals and inspirations of those who have gone before.

JOHN A. WARE,
Associate Director,
Laboratory of Anthropology/
Museum of Indian Arts and Culture

I AM HERE

The Southwest: An Overview

JOHN A. WARE

I AM HERE: TWO THOUSAND YEARS OF SOUTHWEST INDIAN ARTS AND CULTURE traces the evolution of four important southwestern material culture traditions: basketry, textiles, ceramics, and adornment. In exploring the growth and development of these traditions, prehistoric past is connected with historic present, and centuries-old patterns of adaptation and survival in the American Southwest are illustrated.

The cultural traditions here presented belong to the Puebloan and Apachean people, who for centuries have occupied the northern extremities of the Southwest Culture Area, a large region encompassing much of the southwestern United States and northwestern Mexico (see map).

Although the area is noted for its arid climate and physiographic diversity, its boundaries are defined by cultural rather than geographic expressions. To the east in the Great Plains, immediately north in the Great Basin, and in California to the west, hunting and gathering was still the traditional mode of subsistence at the time of European contact. The Southwest was distinguished from these adjacent culture areas by an early commitment to farming—in some cases as a minor supplement to wild foods, in other cases as a major investment in agriculture and all its technical and organizational ramifications.

Farming became part of the southwestern cultural tradition between 2,000 and 3,000 years ago, as domestic plants and farming technologies diffused north into the Southwest from central Mexico. The resident populations that were the recipients of this new way of life were broad-based hunters and gatherers whose ancestors had been exploiting the wild resources of the Southwest since the end of the last glacial epoch, more than 12,000 years ago.

Our knowledge of early southwestern hunter-gatherers is limited, primarily because little material evidence of their culture and their adaptation has survived. If, however, they were at all like arid-land hunters and gatherers who have survived elsewhere into our century, we may surmise that they lived in small, loosely knit, highly mobile bands, following the track of wild game and the flowering and fruiting cycle of wild plants, and that they resumed their wanderings when the local food supply would no longer support them.

The northern Southwest is a land of topographic extremes characterized by deep canyons cut into broad valleys and ringed by high mountains. The early hunter-gatherers undoubtedly exploited the ecological diversity that accompanies such topographic variation, moving frequently to take advantage of seasonal food sources at varying altitudes and exposures. Because they moved so often, they had few material possessions and left little behind. We do know that as the glaciers retreated in the north and as the great herds of Pleistocene megafauna withdrew to the high plains on their way to extinction, early hunters and gatherers turned increasingly to a diet of small animals and wild plants. It is likely that the shift to plant collecting pre-adapted early hunters and gatherers for a later shift to domestic plants and a farming economy.

Corn, squash, and the technologies of planting, hoeing, and harvesting appear to have arrived in the Southwest from Mexico during the first or second millennium B.C. By the beginning of the Christian era, corn and squash plants had been modified to grow in virtually every arable niche in the northern Southwest. A few hundred years later, cotton, another Mex-

Navajo life in Monument Valley, Arizona.
Photograph by Paul Logsdon.

1

ican import, was being grown in the lower desert elevations of the Southwest, and not long after cotton came a protein-rich staple, the common bean.

The advent of farming in the Southwest probably had no immediate impact on the nomadic populations, but eventually it set in motion significant social and economic changes. By providing a reliable yet stationary food source, farming encouraged a once mobile population to move less frequently. As the necessity for migration was lessened, so too was the need for the strict ceilings on family and community size that maintain hunter-gatherer populations at optimum levels well below the carrying capacity of the environment. As population grew, efforts in the fields were intensified and mobility was further curtailed.

The first settled farming communities appeared in the northern Southwest during the first and second centuries A.D. As farming communities evolved, they adapted in specific ways to specific southwestern environments. Regional differences intensified as local adaptations became increasingly fine tuned. By A.D. 500, archaeologists are able to distinguish at least four major formative farming cultures in the northern Southwest, based on differences in settlement pattern, architecture, and material culture and technology.

In the mountains and desert river valleys of western Arizona and extending south to the delta of the Colorado River were the Hakataya farmers, the prehistoric ancestors of the Yuman-speaking tribes of western Arizona. In the fertile desert river valleys of southern Arizona were the Hohokam, whose descendants still practice irrigation farming on the Gila River floodplain south of Phoenix. In the high mountains of eastern Arizona and western New Mexico, south to the mountains and valleys of northern Chihuahua, were the prehistoric Mogollon, whose hunter-gatherer forebears were the first southwestern practitioners of Mexican farming technology. And finally, in the high mesa and canyon country of the Four Corners region, atop the Colorado Plateau, were the Anasazi, ancestors of the modern Pueblo Indians of New Mexico and eastern Arizona. It is to the prehistoric moun-

tain and plateau farmers of New Mexico—the Mogollon and Anasazi—that we now turn our attention.

The earliest Mogollon and Anasazi farming communities consisted of clusters of shallow pit houses on ridgetops overlooking fertile floodplains and alluvial valleys. The establishment of seasonally sedentary farming communities encouraged the proliferation of material culture, and as material possessions increased, so too did the rates of disposal of worn and broken implements in and around human habitations. With permanent settlements also came substantial architecture. The result was an accumulation of occupation debris, much of which has survived into the twentieth century as a rich archaeological record of prehistoric village life in the northern Southwest.

As the population of farming communities grew, technology changed to support it. The introduction of ceramic technology from Mexico in the early centuries of the Christian era was one of the most important innovations. By A.D. 500, pottery was being manufactured and traded throughout the Southwest, and ceramic vessels quickly replaced baskets as the primary technology for food storage and preparation.

Population growth also encouraged rapid changes in architecture and community patterns. By the eighth and ninth centuries A.D., a variety of surface architectural forms began to replace the pit house as the primary form of residential architecture, while a highly stylized pit house, or kiva, was retained for social and ceremonial functions.

In the tenth and eleventh centuries, large villages appeared for the first time in the northern Southwest, some with more than 500 rooms and resident populations estimated in the hundreds. The San Juan Basin of northwestern New Mexico contains the remnants of many large, eleventh-century towns linked by hundreds of miles of linear roadways and supported by extensive agricultural and hydraulic systems.

Many of the large Pueblo villages on the Colorado Plateau and in the highlands of western New Mexico and eastern Arizona were abandoned by the middle of the twelfth century, and there is evidence of regional de-population across the entire northern

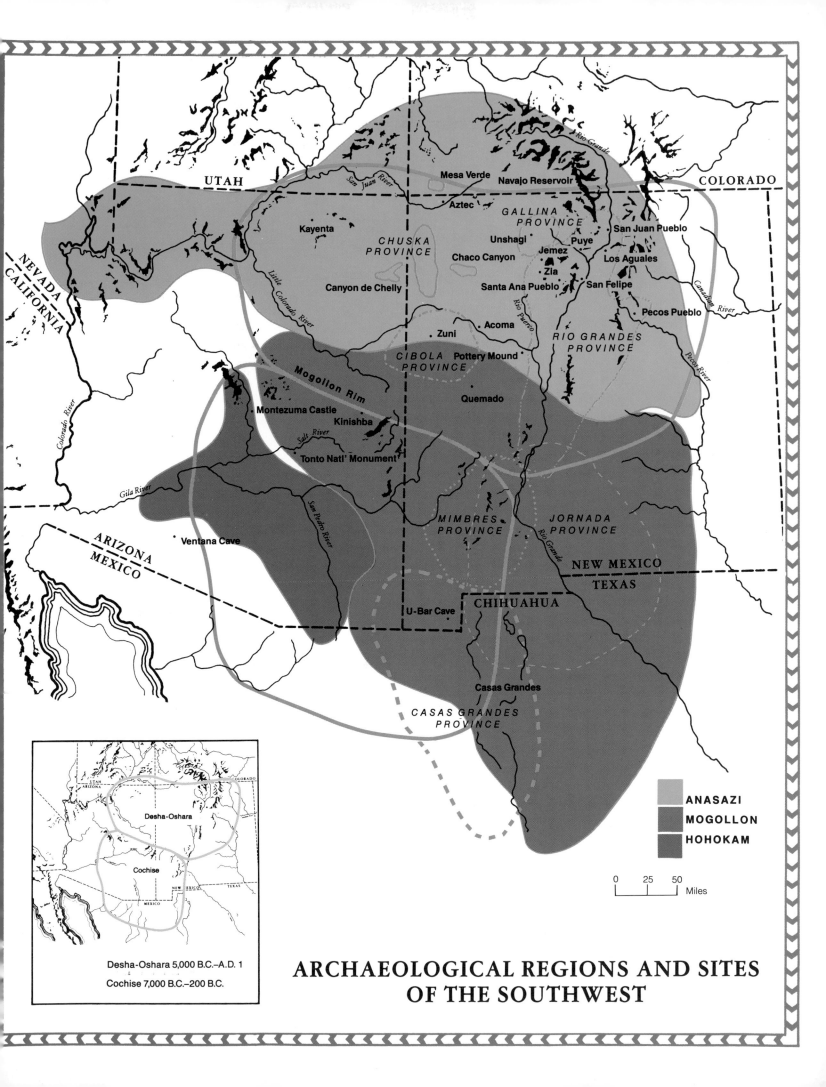

UTAH

COLORADO

NEVADA

CALIFORNIA

Mesa Verde

Navajo Reservoir

Aztec

GALLINA PROVINCE

Kayenta

CHUSKA PROVINCE

Unshagi • Puye • San Juan Pueblo

Jemez • Los Aguales

Chaco Canyon

• Zia

San Felipe

Canyon de Chelly

Santa Ana Pueblo

Pecos Pueblo

Rio Grande

San Juan River

Little Colorado River

Rio Puerco

Canadian River

Pecos River

• Zuni • Acoma

CIBOLA PROVINCE

Pottery Mound •

RIO GRANDES PROVINCE

Mogollon Rim

Quemado

Montezuma Castle

Kinishba

Salt River

Tonto Natl' Monument

Colorado River

Gila River

San Pedro River

MIMBRES PROVINCE

JORNADA PROVINCE

Rio Grande

• Ventana Cave

ARIZONA

MEXICO

NEW MEXICO

TEXAS

U-Bar Cave

CHIHUAHUA

Casas Grandes

CASAS GRANDES PROVINCE

ANASAZI

MOGOLLON

HOHOKAM

0 25 50
Miles

ARCHAEOLOGICAL REGIONS AND SITES
OF THE SOUTHWEST

Southwest. The causes of this collapse have been debated for years. The abandonment of many regions coincided with a major drought episode centered around A.D. 1150, but environmental change rarely provides a satisfactory explanation for such large-scale events and processes. Some archaeologists believe that populations had become so dependent on farming that they lost the ability to adapt to greater-than-normal fluctuations in the temperature and moisture regime of the arid Southwest. Others argue that intensive farming practices of the tenth and eleventh centuries so degraded the regional environment that agricultural potentials declined, forcing the abandonment of marginal farming areas.

Whatever the cause, by the end of the thirteenth century Anasazi and Mogollon farmers had abandoned much of their former range and had aggregated instead in large population centers in well-watered regions of the Mogollon highlands and along perennial watercourses on the periphery of the Colorado Plateau. The Rio Grande and its tributaries in central New Mexico attracted the largest concentration of displaced Pueblo farmers. When Coronado entered New Mexico in 1540 he encountered over 100 occupied Pueblo villages in New Mexico, most of them concentrated along the floodplain of the Rio Grande, from Albuquerque north to Taos.

The Coronado Expedition ushered in the Historic Period in the Rio Grande Valley. Searching for cities of gold, Coronado's party found only the stone and adobe villages of the Pueblo Indians. Early Spanish explorations of the Southwest paved the way for the establishment in 1598 for the first European colony in New Mexico, at a site north of the present town of Española. Twelve years later the capital of the New Mexico colony was moved thirty miles south to Santa Fe, the "City of the Holy Faith."

From the early 1600s onward, the increasing influence and control of the Spanish altered the direction and pace of development of Pueblo Indian culture. The Spanish introduced new domesticated plants and animals, along with metal tools, wheeled vehicles, the plow, firearms, and a new and powerful religion. They introduced, also, European diseases that decimated the indigenous populations, and institutions of economic and religious oppression that resulted in widespread discontent and, eventually, in open revolt against Spanish authority.

The Pueblo Revolt of 1680 was one of the most successful Native American uprisings in the history of European colonization of the New World. It was short-lived, however. In 1692 the Spanish regained their foothold in New Mexico, and for the next 130 years, Spanish domination of the Rio Grande Valley was never seriously challenged.

The Spanish explorers of the 1500s had long been preceded by another group of explorers, this coming from the north. The Apaches, and their linguistic cousins the Navajo, were Athabascan-speaking hunters and gatherers who migrated south from western Canada, arriving in the Southwest, some scholars believe, around A.D. 1400. Perhaps no other southwestern Indian culture would be so radically changed by contact with Europeans.

The introduction of the horse transformed many Apachean bands from hunters and gatherers to specialized raiders bent on exploiting the agricultural surplus of the Pueblo and Spanish farming communities. The intensity of Apachean raiding increased throughout central New Mexico during the 1600s and 1700s. Curiously, the devastating raids on Pueblo and Spanish communities were interspersed with interludes of peaceful trade, when Apache, Pueblo, and Spaniard exchanged ideas as well as material goods and food.

Another Spanish introduction, domesticated sheep, had an equally profound impact on a group of Apacheans from northwestern New Mexico, known locally as the "Apaches de Nabaju" (Apaches of the Cultivated Fields). The addition of sheep husbandry to the Navajo farming and raiding economy led to the early divergence of Navajo and southern Apache culture. Their differences were magnified following the Spanish reconquest of New Mexico in 1692 when many Pueblo peoples, fearful of Spanish reprisals, sought refuge among Navajo bands in northwestern

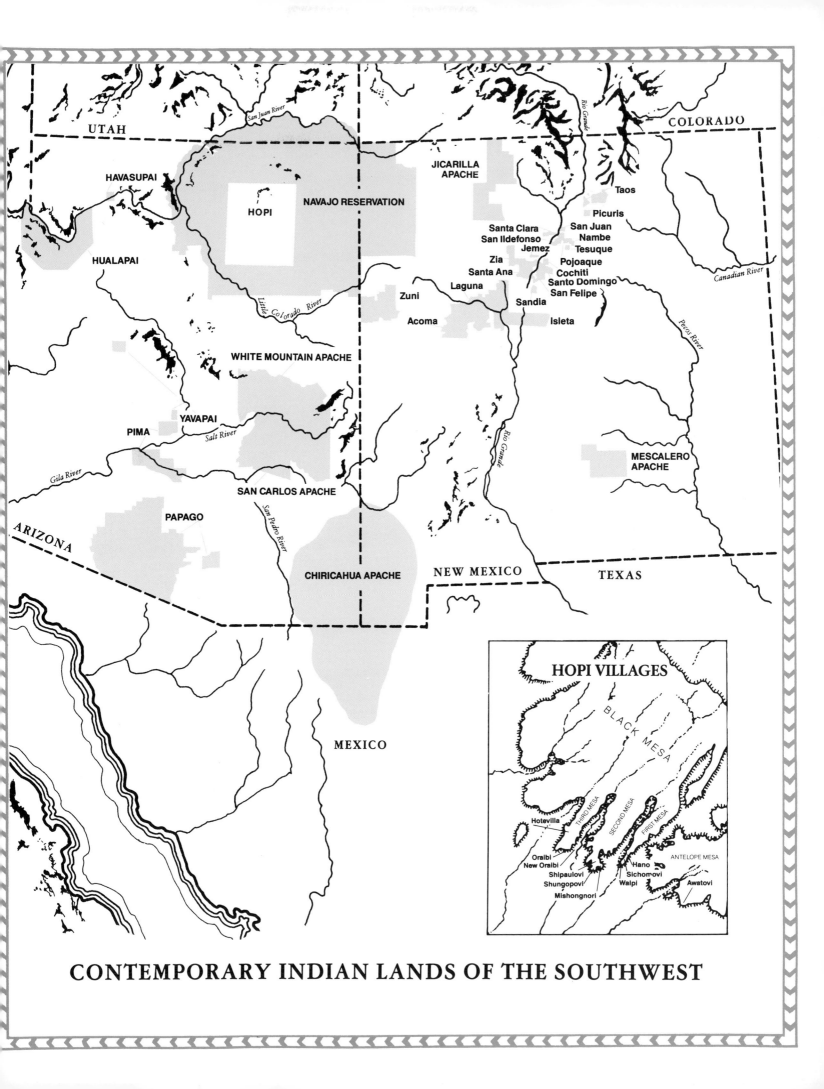

CONTEMPORARY INDIAN LANDS OF THE SOUTHWEST

THE PECOS CLASSIFICATION:
A CHRONOLOGY FOR THE NORTHERN SOUTHWEST

10,000 B.C. PALEO-INDIAN

Pleistocene big-game hunters and gatherers, descendants of immigrants from Asia who crossed the Bering
Straits land bridge into North America at the end of
the Pleistocene.

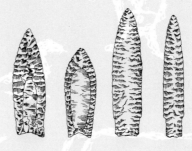

6000 B.C. ARCHAIC

Broad-based hunters and gatherers; corn and squash hor-
ticulture introduced from Mexico during the 1st or 2nd
millennia B.C.

100 B.C. BM II (BASKETMAKER)

The first farming villages appear in northern Southwest; highly mobile, farming and hunting-gathering
populations.

A.D. 400 BM III (BASKETMAKER)

Pit house villages and the earliest evidence of pottery
manufacture; beans and the bow and arrow are introduced.

A.D. 700 PUEBLO I

Shift from pit house to surface architecture and formal village plan; "slipped" pottery and cranial deformation become common.

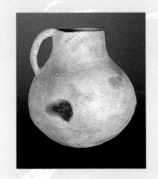

A.D. 900 PUEBLO II

Population growth and settlement dispersal over most of Colorado Plateau; small homestead-type settlements; first large villages appear in San Juan region of New Mexico.

A.D. 1100 PUEBLO III

Period of population mobility, instability, and settlement aggregation leading up to late 13th-century structural collapse.

A.D. 1300 PUEBLO IV

Follows Anasazi abandonment of most of Colorado Plateau; large pueblo population centers in Rio Grande, Little Colorado, and Hopi Mesas.

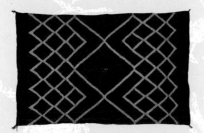

A.D. 1540 PUEBLO V

Historic Pueblo, begins with the Spanish Entrada of 1540 and continues to the present.

New Mexico. During this period of intense contact, the Navajo adopted and modified many Puebloan culture traits, including weaving, a distinctive style of dress, and aspects of Pueblo ritual.

In 1846 the United States Army of the West, under the command of Gen. Stephen Watts Kearny, occupied Santa Fe and claimed the territory of New Mexico for the United States. One of the first priorities of the new regime was to pacify the Navajos and Apaches, whose raids had increased throughout the 1700s and 1800s, leaving large tracts of the northern Southwest virtually uninhabitable. The campaign against the Navajo came to a tragic end in 1864 when more than 7,000 of the tribe, along with some 400 Mescalero Apaches, were rounded up and interned at Bosque Redondo, a small military reservation near Fort Sumner in eastern New Mexico. Known to this day as "The Long Walk," the forced march of the Navajos across New Mexico, and their four years of internment, are still vividly remembered by the Navajo people. Military campaigns against other Apache groups continued into the 1880s.

The Pueblo Indians, though they were not displaced from their land, were not immune to American military force. In 1847 Taos Pueblo rebelled, killing the territory's newly appointed governor, Charles Bent, and mobilizing for an attack on Santa Fe. The United States Army quickly put down the revolt. Another, more insidious form of attack occurred in the late 1800s as pueblos throughout the Rio Grande Valley lost much of their land through the encroachment of Anglo and Hispano squatters. Land encroachment was accompanied by a new cycle of religious persecution, this time at the hands of Protestant missionaries, encouraged and supported by the U.S. government.

The Anglo-American period in New Mexico, following the region's Mexican independence from Spain in 1821, brought drastic economic changes to the eastern, or Rio Grande, pueblos. Beginning in 1821, manufactured goods from the United States, brought into New Mexico over the Santa Fe Trail, began to influence the tastes and habits of the native peoples.

The U.S. military occupation of New Mexico in 1846, and the extension of the railroad into the territory between 1879 and 1885, vastly increased the volume of American imports. As a result, Indian material culture underwent irrevocable changes. Weaving, for example, died out among the eastern Pueblos, who now had ready access to inexpensive cotton and woolen cloth. Pottery, for home use, declined with the introduction and proliferation of inexpensive metal, crockery, and porcelain items. As new building materials and tools were accepted, milled lumber and iron hardware appeared in Pueblo doorways and sheet glass replaced selenite in windows.

Arts and crafts, suddenly more profitable with the advent of tourism, found a ready market at the railroad stations and the trading posts along Route 66. Within just a few decades after the arrival of the railroad, the economic base of the Pueblos shifted from subsistence farming to wage work and the manufacture of arts and crafts.

Accelerating culture change has all but overtaken the native people of the northern Southwest in the twentieth century. Education, now almost universally available and accepted, is perhaps the single greatest force moving Southwest Indians into the mainstream of American culture. But these changes aside, the Indian cultures of the Southwest have remained living, dynamic societies. Successful legal action has resulted in the compensation for or return of much of the Pueblo land lost to encroachment in the late 1800s. Indian populations have rebounded in this century, approaching or surpassing pre-Spanish population levels. The most recent census figures for the Navajo Nation indicate that the population of North America's largest Indian tribe has passed the 200,000 mark.

Southwestern Indians have demonstrated the uncommon capacity to discriminate among the kinds of changes that they are willing to accept, and to reject many changes that are inconsistent with their values and world views. The ability to adapt centuries-old traditions to a changing world and retain a strong sense of place, function, and context is demonstrated in the traditions that are described and illustrated in what follows. Most of the objects illustrated here are beautiful, and many are priceless, but they are treasures not because of any intrinsic monetary value. Some 300 objects were selected from over 50,000 objects in the collections of the Laboratory of Anthropology. Some were chosen because they are unique or extremely rare; others because they are very old, or perhaps were the first of their kind; still others because they are excellent representative examples of a type of object or a style of manufacture. All the objects have stories to tell about the people and the cultures that produced them, which is, ultimately, why we cherish them as treasures.

Pueblo and Athabascan
Baskets in the Southwest

ANDREW HUNTER WHITEFORD

San Felipe-on-the-Mesa and modern San Felipe Pueblo in
north-central New Mexico. Photograph by Paul Logsdon.

LONG AFTER THE PALEO-INDIANS and the great Ice Age animals they hunted had disappeared from the American Southwest, other peoples began to move into the region. The first Archaic hunters came from the Great Basin to the north around 6,000 B.C. They were nomads who hunted deer, antelope, and other animals and also gathered fruits, nuts, roots, and many kinds of seeds. Pottery was unknown to them, but they brought with them an ancient tradition of basket weaving, in which baskets were employed for food preparation, storage, and portage. This craft tradition formed the basis for the sophisticated complex of basket making that was passed on later to the descendants of the Archaic people, who, in the following centuries, developed into the Anasazi ("Ancient Ones"), known first as the Basketmakers and, eventually, as the Pueblos.

The first baskets used by the Archaic people were shallow trays and carrying baskets made by twining. However, this technique was soon succeeded by coiling (see diagrams), probably because the coiled trays were more efficient for parching and winnowing the small seeds that were a major part of the people's diet. The seeds were collected in baskets, parched, and then ground between stones to make flour for mush and tortillas. Watertight baskets were used to cook soup or stew by heating stones in the fire and then dropping them into the mixture in the basket until it boiled. The first coiled baskets were made with shingle rods of willow or sumac stitched together with interlocking wood splints (see diagram). These one-rod baskets continued to be made for thousands of years because they were strong and easy to produce.

While the early people of the Desha-Oshara Archaic Culture occupied the northern part of the Southwest, another group of hunters moved up from below the Rio Grande. These people of the Cochise Archaic Culture were also hunters and basketmakers, but their baskets were different from the ones made in the north. They were coiled with bundles of beargrass or yucca fiber and sewn together with the same materials. Each stitch typically was passed through the stitch in the previous coil, splitting it in two (see diagram). Between 2,000 B.C. and A.D. 1 these were

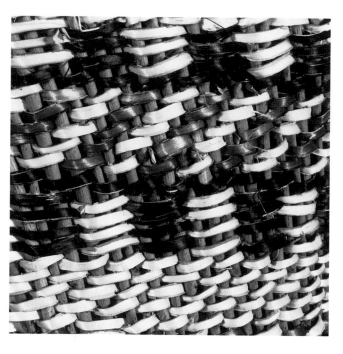

The twining technique involves twisting two or more horizontal elements as they are woven in and out of more rigid vertical elements, called warps.

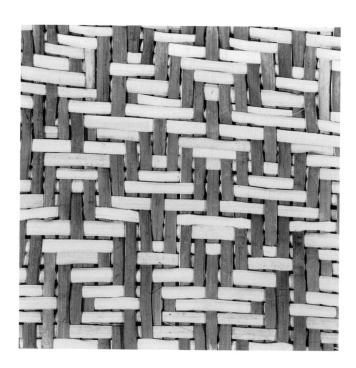

The plaiting technique makes use of a single element or sets of elements that pass over and under each other in a manner similar to that used in textile weaving.

In coiling, the predominant technique used in Southwest basket making, bundles of grass, wood rods, or other materials are wrapped with narrow ribbons and coiled in a continuous spiral.

Hopi basket maker, ca. 1900, demonstrating the coiling technique. Photograph by Carl N. Werntz. Basket illustrations from *Traditions in Transition*, by Barbara Mauldin.

the most common baskets made in the south, but others were coiled with a bundle and a rod (fig. 2).

By 3,000 B.C., the Archaic peoples were distributed over most of the Southwest, where they developed a number of regional cultures. Primitive types of maize, beans, and squash, spreading northward from Mexico, provided the basis for the later growth of farming in the region. Basketry flourished during these early centuries and the Archaic people invented or perfected most of the techniques for making baskets that have been used by their descendants in the Southwest.

By late Archaic times coiling was done with foundations of fiber bundles, with single rods, and with bundles with rod cores, stacked rods, single rods, multiple rods, and a variety of complex and ornate stitching techniques that did not persist into historic times. Fine twined baskets continued to be made, and plaiting (see diagram), another new basketry technique, reached the Southwest from Mexico. Strips of yucca leaves or other materials were woven over and under each other to make shallow trays, sifters, and other forms as well as fine mats. Plaiting spread into the north, and by A.D. 400 to 700 fine ring baskets were being made by the advanced Basketmaker III people (figs. 4, 5). These simple but very useful baskets persisted relatively unchanged into modern times.

THE ANASAZIS

In the northern part of the Southwest the nomadic foragers of the Desha-Oshara Archaic Culture gradually developed into the earliest members of the new and long-lasting Anasazi culture. Known as the Basketmakers because of their skill in this craft, they created settled pit-house villages and became the first farmers of the region between 100 B.C. and A.D. 700. The seeds for their crops came from the early Mogollon Culture, which developed from the Cochise Archaic in the south-central mountains. The stimulus for their pottery, weaving, and jewelry probably came from the same source. In the Cochise-Mogollon area several types of coiled baskets were made: the

13

fiber bundle type, which reflected the Mexican influence; and also baskets coiled with two rods and a small fiber bundle—a technique which originated in the late Oshara Archaic, spread over most of the Southwest, and became the dominant type of coiling throughout Anasazi history.

The Basketmaker people developed basket weaving to an impressive level of beauty and technological sophistication. They coiled large conical burden baskets in various techniques and decorated them with elaborate red and black designs. They also made trays and bowls, sometimes using complex coiling techniques, such as stitch-and-wrap, that were not preserved by later peoples.

Toward the end of the Basketmaker period a special type of burden basket appeared which seems to have had ceremonial significance. These rare baskets were wedge-shaped, with narrow oval bases and straight flaring sides, and were much smaller then the conical carriers. They were made with two-rod and bundle coils and decorated with geometric designs of black and red dyed splints. Their small size, no more than twelve inches in height (compared with the conical carriers, which measured up to thirty-six inches in diameter), indicates that they were not made to carry much. The small clay effigies of female figures often found with these wedge-shaped baskets emphasize their ritual status.

An important example of a ceremonial basket in the collection of the Laboratory of Anthropology was excavated in 1960 by Lambert and Ambler at U-Bar Cave in the Alamo Hueco Mountains of southern New Mexico (fig. 39). The presence of many ritual objects, such as an altar of arrow shafts at the entrance, many painted wooden prayer sticks, and a well-preserved wooden painted kachina figure, indicates that the cave served ceremonial purposes. The basket was found in a pit with an enormous net (151 feet long) woven of human hair bundled in its mouth and the pelts of two ring-tailed cats carefully placed inside it. The excavators noted that "superficially, it is somewhat reminiscent of bifurcated and wedge-shaped carrying baskets of the Basket Maker—Pueblo culture" (Lambert and Ambler, 1961), but they were reluctant to identify the basket with the Basketmaker III people and with an early date of approximately A.D. 500. The broad encircling zigzag band of red-brown dyed splints edged with black on the U-Bar Cave basket is different from the complex geometric red and black panels that decorate the front and back surfaces of the Basketmaker III carriers from northern Arizona. It differs from them also in being stitched with yucca splints instead of willow or sumac.

The ceremonial burden basket is certainly old and it is difficult to dismiss its similarity to the Basketmaker III baskets. Its condition indicates that it had seen a great deal of use before it was buried in U-Bar Cave. It shows abrasion from wear and the base is bent out of shape and badly broken in at least two places. The ancient people made an effort to repair the breaks by lacing broad splints of willow across them. These repairs obviously were done long after the basket was made and after it had been used for many years, or perhaps centuries.

If this basket is not related to the Basketmaker baskets it would have to be a freak whose unique characteristics were produced independently, which seems unlikely. On the other hand, if it is a variant of the Basketmaker carriers, and if it should be dated with them around A.D. 500, two conclusions seem possible. (1) It is an old basket that was carefully preserved for ritual use until it was buried in the pit at U-Bar Cave some time around A.D. 1300 to 1400. (2) The basket, and some of the other materials, belong to an early occupation of the cave, which may be as old as A.D. 500 to 800. Carbon dating, or some other process, ultimately may provide a date for the basket, but it probably will not determine whether it was made by the people who carried it into the U-Bar Cave for hunting rites or rather was an antique heirloom they had preserved carefully for such use.

The Basketmakers also sealed some of their early water jars by coating baskets with hot piñon pitch, another of the early techniques that continued in use in the Southwest for centuries. One large jar (fig. 42) was found in a cave in the Jemez Mountains. It was coiled with a single rod and sewn with interlocking stitches. Red clay was smeared between the stitches

Prehistoric Basket Tray, 700–800. Found in a cave in the Guadalupe Mountains of New Mexico, this coiled basket is sewn with beargrass and decorated at the rim with yucca root.

Early Historic Pueblo Basket, 1700–1850. A fine example of a two-rod-and-bundle coiled basket.

before the pitch coating was applied to the inside and outside surfaces. The herringbone rim seen on this basket was first used by the early Basketmakers.

Another typical water jar, which also was coated with clay and pitched inside and out (fig. 32), was constructed by twining and has two carved wooden handles to which a carrying strap was attached. It was found in a cave in the Lukachukai Mountains and represents a style of water jar that continued to be made and used by the Navajos, Paiutes, and Western Apaches until recent times.

PUEBLO BASKETS

By A.D. 800 farming was firmly established in the Southwest and the people settled in increasingly large villages, where they developed complex religio-ceremonial rituals and perfected the arts of architecture, lapidary work, weaving, and pottery. The transition to open villages from sheltered caves (except at sites like Mesa Verde) produced conditions that were not favorable for the preservation of organic materials, and pottery largely replaced baskets for both ceremonial and daily use. This did not mean that baskets were no longer made; some of the most elegant baskets ever produced in the Southwest were created by the Pueblo people. Their coiled baskets were even more finely stitched than those of the preceding Basketmakers, and they decorated their trays and bowls with complex geometric designs in red and black dyed stitches. Two decorated baskets from the Hospitibito area in Arizona demonstrate that large burden baskets, some of a special funnel-like shape, were used as late as Pueblo III (A.D. 1100 to 1300) (Haury, 1945). Few examples of Pueblo carrying baskets have been preserved, but it is possible that they may have been more common than present evidence indicates.

The most unusual Pueblo carriers were exotic ceremonial baskets which possibly developed from the old Basketmaker wedge-shaped baskets. They were small, often beautifully decorated, and made with bases that were so deeply indented that two "legs" were formed. These baskets must have possessed ritual significance because they were found with small clay effigies of similar baskets and of women, and their peculiar shape served no utilitarian function. No remnants of this ceremonial complex are known from the historic Pueblos.

Materials excavated at Antelope House in northeast Arizona and other sites revealed that a wide range of coiling techniques was used by the Pueblo people. Two-rod and bundle coils and single rod coils were the most popular, but they also made baskets with fiber bundle coils, two stacked rods with a welt, five bunched rods, two stacked rods, and three rods in a triangular bunch. New basket forms were produced and some were decorated with zones of ornamental stitch-and-wrap coiling. At Pueblo Bonito and other late Pueblo villages, baskets were found covered with mosaic designs of turquoise and other materials, while bird quills were worked into the designs of others.

Especially during the Pueblo III period, the twill-plaited yucca ring basket flourished. Some were very plain and simple with narrow splints evenly woven (fig. 86), but most were twill-plaited to produce all-over patterns of concentric diamonds, transverse zigzag bands, crosses, and complicated menders and interlocking figures. The designs were often intensified by dying some splints black. Most trays were finished by plaiting the splint ends into elaborate braids just below the rims.

HISTORIC PUEBLO BASKETS

There is very little information about the baskets the Pueblo peoples made and used at the end of the Prehistoric Period and during the Early Historic Period of white contact. The first soldiers and missionaries in the Southwest rarely collected or described baskets, and it was not until ethnological research began that specific information about Pueblo basketry became available. When Cushing and Matilda and James Stevenson went to Zuni and Hopi in 1879 they collected baskets; the Hemenway Expedition of 1890 to 1894 acquired the Hopi collection gathered

between 1875 and 1890 by the trader Thomas Keam; and Mennonite missionary/ethnologist H. R. Voth collected a wealth of materials from the Hopis while he lived with them from 1893 into the twentieth century. In addition to these collections, baskets are depicted in many of the photographs taken by A. C. Vroman, J. K. Hillers, George Wharton James, Ben Wittick, and others. Comparison of the baskets from these sources with those made in recent years reveals a remarkable degree of consistency and conservatism.

Hopi baskets from the Sallie Wagner collection, 1930s–1950s. The continuity of Hopi basket making may be traced from the 1880s through the 1930s, '40s, and '50s into contemporary practice. Photograph by Andrew Whiteford.

HOPI BASKETS

In 1890 the women of the villages on Second Mesa were making coiled baskets and those on Third Mesa were producing plaited wicker baskets, just as they do today. The coiled plaques collected in the 1890s were made with galleta grass bundles, sewn with close stitches of yucca splints, and decorated with both subtle natural colors and brilliant commercial dyes. The geometric designs were more sparse than on modern baskets, but kachina figures (fig. 76) and eagles were almost identical with plaques made today. Although it often is said that early Hopi coiled baskets always were made with large, loose coils (fig. 76), many baskets in the early collections have tight, narrow coils. In addition to plaques, which frequently were used in dances and weddings, the nineteenth-century Hopis also made deep basket bowls (fig. 129), and some very large, deep baskets, sometimes fitted with lids, were usually decorated with full-figure kachinas or eagles and rain clouds (figs. 153, 154).

During the first half of the twentieth century basket making on Second Mesa continued with relatively little change. Brilliant, gaudy commercial dyes became popular for a while, but the weavers eventually returned to the old natural materials for most of their colors. Techniques and materials remained the same, but coils generally became slimmer and sewing became so tight and precise that the stitches seem to interlock. The old designs were often used, but their execution became more dense and more complex, and details on kachina figures were usually emphasized with overstitching. The very large deep baskets were rarely made, but other bowls were richly decorated with ornate kachinas and full figures or heads of pronghorn antelopes (figs. 114, 129).

In the final decades of the nineteenth century and probably long before, the Hopi women in the villages of Third Mesa wove plaited wicker baskets with rabbit brush and sumac. The baskets in the early collections are almost identical with those made today and they were probably used in the same ways. The colors made with vegetal and mineral compounds, principally red, yellow, blue, brown, and black, were not as brilliant as the commercial dyes used for a short time toward the end of the century. Designs consisted of kachinas, eagles (fig. 55), whirlwinds (fig. 167), and abstract geometric patterns, many with special names and significance. Some undecorated plaited wicker baskets also were made and, like the colored baskets, were bound around their edges with strips of yucca leaf.

The brightly colored plaited wicker baskets made in the twentieth century continue the early tradition with little change. They still are sold for income and are frequently used in ceremonies. Symbolic patterns and old kachina figures (fig. 128), whirlwind motifs,

Young Hopi basketmakers from Shipaulovi Village, Second Mesa, Arizona. Early 1900s. Photo Archives, Museum of New Mexico.

butterflies, and spread-winged eagles still are common, and deep baskets probably are more common now than at an earlier time. The Hopis are one of the most productive basket-making tribes in the country.

Yucca ring-baskets were important household utensils for the Hopis in prehistoric times, and they still are made and used in most villages. Some of the old ones were made in plain plaiting with very narrow splints, but most were twill-plaited like the modern ones, with the splints compressed or spaced apart to make sifting trays. They are generally shallow, with allover patterns of interlocking frets, labyrinths, and concentric figures, often highlighted with yucca splints of diverse natural shades obtained from different sections of the plant or by bleaching the leaves in the sun. Distinctive colored ring-baskets are also made by dying some of the splints black or red.

Traditional Hopi burden baskets were plaited with sumac or willow shoots, with the bark left on. They were generally rough and serviceable, with unbound rims and no decoration. Some were large and made to carry loads of wood, corn, or fruit on the bearer's back. Smaller ones, generally called "peach baskets," were finished a little more carefully and used in dances. Large oblong baskets reinforced with U-shaped rods of juniper were made to be hung on the sides of burros. For obvious reasons burden baskets are now rarely made, although some, generally old ones, are carried by certain kachinas in the dances.

A distinctive type of plaited wicker basket still made and used by the Hopis is the piki tray used to hold the rolls of paper-thin corn bread (piki) prepared for ceremonial occasions and is usually flat and rectangular. The center section is twill-plaited with groups of dunebroom stems and the wide border is plain plaited with wefts of sumac crossing the dunebroom shoots that protrude from the center. At the rim the ends of the shoots are bent together and bound with yucca splints.

ZUNI AND ACOMA

Although the basket-making tradition has not survived at Zuni as it has among the Hopis, we know that many baskets were made and used there before the turn of the century. The Stevensons collected more than 150 baskets and carefully recorded their functions in parching seeds, carrying water, holding sacred meal for dances, gathering and caging locusts, carrying fruit, holding peaches, storing treasures, washing corn, sifting ashes from toasted corn, and storing medicine (Stevenson 1884). Many of the baskets were twined jars and bottles, often covered with pitch, but there were also some very fine coiled baskets, generally small bowls with incurved rims or little *ollas* (jars). These last are especially important because examples are to be found in many collections, where they usually are misidentified. The Zunis called these small coiled vase-shaped baskets "treasure baskets" and used them to hold sacred meal for dances (fig. 43). Their narrow coils have two-rod and bundle foundations and are tightly stitched with fine wood splints. The flaring rim of the *olla* has a flat lip finished with herringbone stitching. This, and also the netted design of black and red dyed stitches, is typical of these baskets. Though the upper section of the basket seen in figure 43 is missing, the black design of rectangular

Hopi Third Mesa Plaited Wicker Basket, 1925.

Hopi Third Mesa Basket, 1927.

Hopi Yucca Ring Basket, 1954, made at Mishongnovi, Second Mesa, by Dinah Jay.

18

meanders shows plainly on the body. When baskets of this kind were collected at Zuni, Hopi, Zia, and other pueblos in the 1890s they were already old, and the Indians said that they were no longer being made. Their actual age is unknown, but they deserve to be known as Old Pueblo baskets, a title bestowed on them by Mason (1904) and endorsed later by Weltfish and Morris and Burgh.

The Stevensons collected one large and several small burden baskets from Zuni, but they are not described. Little is known about carrying baskets from any pueblos other than Hopi. For this reason three specimens collected at Acoma may be important in providing some information about the Early Historic Period. Two of them were found in 1961 under the floor of an old house; the other was collected at Acoma by Kenneth Chapman (photos, right). They resemble Apache burden baskets in shape and they have been regarded as examples of trade with that tribe. But they differ from the burden baskets of the Western Apaches in a number of ways. One of them (top) has two U-shaped reinforcing rods, like most Apache baskets, but these are lacking in the other two baskets. The baskets are twined with sumac or willow splints, an unusual technique in Pueblo culture. One is woven entirely in plain twine (bottom) except for areas of three-strand twining at the base and below the rim. The other baskets are worked in a combination of plain and twill twine with the strands given a half-twist to turn the darker bark surface toward the exterior to form the design. This process is very rare in traditional Apache baskets. The most distinctive features are the rims, which are finished with a single rod. Below the rim the ends of the warps are bent to the side and plaited over and under the three or four adjacent warps. Finally, the rim rod is lashed to the bent warps with strips of skin. The most elaborate design consists of a band of light interlocking diamonds separated by heavy black bands. There are other details that make these baskets unique, but it will suffice to note that several similar baskets in the Arizona State Museum were collected by a trader who lived at Zuni, and there are a number in the collection of the School of Amer-

Three Pueblo twined burden baskets, 1850–1880. All were collected at Acoma Pueblo.

ican Research in Santa Fe that are noted to have come from Acoma. There are probably others buried in Apache collections around the country.

THE RIO GRANDE PUEBLOS

There exists little material evidence for the early history of basketry in the Rio Grande pueblos, although we know that baskets were being made here before and during the nineteenth century. It appears that the only type of basket made here over any length of time was the ancient yucca ring basket. These baskets still are made today at Cochiti, Jemez, and possibly other villages. Although these closely resemble Hopi ring-baskets they are often deeper, the yucca fringe around the rim is longer, and groups of yucca splints, instead of single splints as in Hopi baskets, are plaited across each other. Also, concentric squares are preferred to the complex labyrinths and interlocking figures used at Hopi, and there are no colored designs.

Because these villages are part of the Anasazi tradition it may be assumed that they made coiled baskets at one time, but the evidence is sparse. The survey directed by Ellis in 1959 (Ellis and Walpole 1949) located old coiled baskets at Jemez, Zia, Santa Ana, San Felipe, Santa Clara, and San Juan. They were made with coils of two-rod and bundle, one rod, two rods, and three rods. Many of the baskets had been obtained in trade, but a number of worn specimens were identified by the owners as having been made in the villages in which they were found, and sometimes by members of the family, at times ranging from 1890 to 1956. Some were plain, others were decorated with red block crosses, encircling red bands with zigzag edges, and red and black stepped lines.

Basket Dance at San Ildefonso Pueblo, 1920. Most of the baskets are
Jicarilla Apache. Photograph by Sheldon Parsons. Photo Archives,
Museum of New Mexico.

All the makers, when they could be identified, were men, and the only coiled baskets made in recent years in the Rio Grande pueblos were made at Jemez by the men of the Gachupin family. The relationship of the Gachupin baskets to the Pueblo tradition is difficult to assess because, like the Jicarilla Apaches, they use a five-rod coil foundation and one man of the family has stated that his father learned the craft from a Jicarilla woman. However, Ellis reported that the father learned from a man who had learned from a Navajo family.

The only other kind of basket made in the Rio Grande pueblos is also made by men. These baskets are referred to as willow wicker baskets and they have been made in these villages at least since the late nineteenth century. Their origins are problematical. They are regarded as derived from European (Spanish, Mexican) sources because similar baskets occur in non-Indian cultures. However, the wicker plaiting technique, the use of willow shoots, and the basic rim treatment replicate old Pueblo traditions. Almost all these willow baskets are bowls, some shallow and others quite deep (fig. 102). The slender stems, still covered with their red or maroon bark, are plaited in groups under and over spokes of willow or sumac on the bottoms and warps consisting of bunches of slender willow withes on the sides. At the rim the warps, by being bent in a graceful arc and plaited diagonally back through six or seven adjacent sets of warps, form the distinctive feature of these baskets: a lacy scalloped rim. To terminate the weaving the warp ends are gathered on the outer surface and braided into a reinforcing ridge or flange. For decoration simple white bands are created by scraping off the bark. At one time large baskets of this type were made at San Ildefonso and San Juan, and some are still being made at Cochiti and Santo Domingo.

NAVAJO BASKETS

The baskets of these Athabascan-speaking people, who came into the Southwest long after the pueblos were established, are described here because it seems certain that the Navajos learned basket making, as well as weaving and other arts, from the Pueblos. Perhaps when the two peoples were living together after the Pueblo Revolt and the Reconquest of 1692–96, the Navajos learned to make baskets with two-rod and bundle coils in the traditional Anasazi way. This was the basic technique in Navajo basket making at least until the final quarter of the nineteenth century, when textile weaving superseded basket making among the Navajo.

Early Navajo baskets were mostly shallow bowls made with narrow coils sewn with sumac splints. They are thin-walled, smooth, and finished with a flat herringbone rim. Red equilateral crosses outlined with black, called Spider Woman Crosses, were common decorations, but even more common were encircling broad red bands edged with black triangles, crosses, or right-angled flags (figs. 53, 54). An important design that was rare in these old two-rod and bundle baskets was the wedding basket pattern, in which the red band is bordered on both sides with black triangles and a light-colored star is formed at the center. Baskets were required for the many rituals so important in Navajo life and on each basket the red encircling band was carefully split to form a narrow "pathway" at the point where the final coil ends. This enabled the medicine men or singers to orient the baskets properly in the darkened hogan during a ceremony by running their fingers around the rim.

Although it is often said that the Navajos had abandoned basket making by the turn of the century, many women, particularly on the eastern end of the reservation, continued to make baskets. It is true that, in some manner which has never been explained, the Navajos arranged to have their baskets made by the Southern Utes and the San Juan Paiutes. The Paiutes adopted the most important design, which was the wedding basket pattern, and they produced quantities of these baskets for many years. For some reason the Navajos did not require the Paiutes to make baskets for them with two-rod and bundle coils, or perhaps they prohibited them from making them in this way. The baskets made by the Paiutes were coiled with three rods in a triangular bunch and they were considerably heavier and stiffer than traditional Navajo baskets. This type of coiling was not traditional among the Paiutes.

In early days and well into the twentieth century, the Navajos made many coiled waterjars (fig. 91), pitched inside and out like the old Pueblo water carriers, in various shapes and sizes for use and for trade.

In the 1960s a renaissance in Navajo basket making occurred when classes were organized at Navajo Community College and other institutions to teach Navajo women how to make baskets. By 1973 at least one hundred basketmakers were at work, providing baskets for their own people and selling them in the trading posts. There seems to have been little interest in reviving traditional Navajo weaving techniques or designs, with the result that most of the baskets had heavy coils, often with foundations of five rods, like the baskets of the Jicarilla Apaches. Designs sometimes followed traditional patterns but, particularly in the northwestern part of the Navajo reservation, in the vicinity of Navajo Mountain and Oljato, the weavers created many new and original designs. Extremely large baskets were made and also many miniatures, decorated with bird figures, whirlwinds, a

variety of geometric patterns, and endless variations on the traditional wedding basket. Several women, possibly stimulated by the work of Sally Black of Mexican Hat, copied designs from textiles and introduced *yei* figures (Navajo supernatural beings) into their baskets. Other women, in the vicinity of Monument Valley, copied Hopi kachina figures. The range of concepts copied and explored by these Navajo basketmakers seems endless and it is impossible to predict the direction they may take in the future.

Not all the work done by modern Navajo basketmakers is highly inventive or carefully executed. Some make only wedding baskets. Others produce rather crude, lightly pitched water jars, unlike the traditional water jars—small, triangular baskets coiled with three stacked rods or with bundles of wood splints and sewn with widely separated stitches. They are neither functional nor decorative, but they are easy to make and apparently they find buyers.

In the area near Farmington, on the eastern end of the reservation, one woman makes large jars with globular bodies, neatly coiled with stacked rods, covered with a smooth coat of amber piñon pitch, and embellished with thick braided horsehair carrying loops. These are superior products.

Yavapai basketmaker Bessie Mike, taken at Ft. McDowell, Arizona, 1983. Photographs by Andrew Whiteford.

THE APACHES

These Athabascan-speaking tribes are relatives of the Navajos who migrated into the Southwest from western Canada some time between A.D. 1200 and 1500. The time is indeterminate, but it is clear that they had spread over most of the Southwest by the late sixteenth and early seventeenth centuries and had become separate tribal entities by the early eighteenth century. Two tribes emerged in New Mexico, the Jicarilla Apaches in the north and the Mescaleros in the south. In southern Arizona several tribal groups are combined as the Western Apaches. In spite of military persecution and dislocation these people maintained their cultural integrity and today are beginning to prosper. Their life patterns differ considerably from each other and baskets played a more important role than pottery in their lives. Their earlier uses were for gathering and preparing food, carrying burdens and children, and service in the ceremonials. After the railroad arrived, baskets became the Apaches' most important productions for sale to tourists and collectors. This brought about changes in the craft but also created a reason for its continuation. Each of the Apache tribes made baskets that differed greatly from those made by the other groups.

THE JICARILLA APACHES

Early association with the Pueblo peoples of the upper Rio Grande altered the basically Plains Indian pattern of the Jicarillas' lives. One of the skills they learned from their neighbors was basketry, and they became so skilled in the making of fine coiled baskets that the Pueblos abandoned the craft and filled their need for baskets by trading with the Jicarillas.

Little is known about the basket-making techniques that were transmitted to the Jicarillas, but it is known that baskets coiled with both three- and five-rod bundles were made at one time by the Pueblos. The earliest known Jicarilla baskets are stout trays or bowls with five-rod coil foundations, sewn with splints of sumac and finished at the rim with herringbone stitching. This is the kind of basket still

Apache woman with baskets, ca. 1900. Photo Archives, Museum of New Mexico.

made by Jicarilla women. In the nineteenth century they were decorated with separated geometric figures and occasional representations of horses in subtle natural tans and browns. By 1890, when commercial dyes became available, Jicarilla basketry exploded in brilliant and gaudy colors. Red, yellow, blue, green, purple, orange, and other colors were combined, but fortunately they faded quickly into more muted hues (fig. 131). The use of these bright colors persisted until the 1980s, when some of the basketmakers began experimenting with natural colors.

The serviceable nature of Jicarilla baskets was apparent to the wives of farmers and ranchers in their area and the Apaches began, possibly at their request, to produce large basket trays with opposed handles for carrying laundry (fig. 131) and also large cylindrical laundry hampers with lids (fig. 111). The

Jicarillas responded to the strange tastes of the eastern visitors by also creating some strange and unusual baskets such as coiled "straw" hats (fig. 110), pitcher shapes with loop handles, unique jars with tall ring bases, and bowls with open fretwork around the rims, to be used as sewing baskets (fig. 69). These nontraditional forms were abandoned after a few years and during a period of extreme poverty between 1905 and 1920 basketry almost died out. Today it is an active craft still producing the large shallow trays as well as occasional deep bowls and traditional water jars.

The tribe maintains a cultural center where some of the women work and their baskets are displayed and sold. The current quality of work is excellent, due in part to the influence of women like Tanzania Pesata, who helped revive basket making in the 1960s, introducing new designs of deer, butterflies, and plants and making fine baskets with narrow three-rod coils. She remembered how to make the traditional water jars, and some of them are still being produced today. They are unique, with globular bodies and rather long necks, and are pitched only on the interior. The outer surface usually is coated with white clay and decorated with groups of short buckskin thongs sometimes threaded with large glass beads. The carrying loops are braided or wrapped horsehair and many of the old jars are decorated with vertical lines of overstitching.

THE MESCALERO APACHES

Very unusual baskets were made by the Mescaleros of southern New Mexico. They were coiled with two willow or sumac rods, one stacked on top of the other, and surmounted with a thin bundle of yucca or bear grass fibers. These wide flat coils were sewn with stitches of yucca leaf or bear grass that passed through the fiber bundle of the previous coil and split the stitches below. As a result of the splitting, the stitches were half-interlocked. The use of yucca stitches and the habit of splitting them deliberately is an old trait in this area, although it is impossible to trace or even to suggest any connection between the Mescaleros and the very early people who first made baskets of this

kind. Perhaps some baskets were preserved until the Mescaleros entered the region. The unusual stacked coiling is also difficult to explain although it occurred at Ventana Cave during the Cochise Archaic, and in scattered other locations.

During the nineteenth century the Mescaleros made coiled jars and other forms, but later production was confined to shallow, bowl-shaped trays decorated predominantly with large radiating lobed petal designs and less frequently with frets, spirals, and, rarely, figures of men and animals. Baskets used in ceremonies were required to have patterns with four petals or other elements (fig. 92); designs with five petals were deliberately designed for sale. The patterns on these baskets were created by using leaf strips from different parts of the plant in use to procure tan, yellow, light green, and almost white colors. Dark red accents or outlines were made with segments of yucca root.

Mescalero Burden Basket, 1910–1920, worked in twilled twine except for a band of three-strand twining near the bottom.

Even more unusual than the stacked rod coiled trays were the deep, straight-sided "boxes" with lids that were coiled with foundations of wide, thin slats of wood. The slats are sometimes one inch in width and approximately one-eighth of an inch thick. Generally they were made of willow or Gambel's oak in a process of which the people say today: "the old people were able to do things we can't do, and they had more patience." The splints apparently were split and then scraped and rubbed with abrasive until they were smooth and even. These splints were usually topped with the usual bundle of fibers and the stitches pass through them. The covered boxes vary in size and are both round and oval in shape with flat bottoms and fitted lids. They are decorated, like the trays, with diamonds, crosses, and broad zigzag bands.

The twined burden baskets of the Mescaleros, and also their relatives the Chiricahuas, were usually cylindrical and twill twined with sumac or willow splints. The baskets generally lacked U-shaped reinforcing rods, had single rod rims, and were decorated with a row of tin cones hung on skin thongs just below the rim and near the base. Some baskets had red and blue bands of dyed splints and some had base patches of buckskin or rawhide.

In the 1980s the only remaining basketmakers among the Mescaleros are two Chiricahua sisters who make twined burden baskets decorated with the colors of felt-tipped ink markers and vertical fringed strips of the kind common to burden baskets of the Western Apaches. Basket making is no longer taught in the craft center, but some women remember how to coil baskets and they could become active again.

THE WESTERN APACHES

Some of the most elaborately designed and technically admirable baskets made in the Southwest were produced by the Western Apaches. Their coiled baskets were made with three smoothed willow or sumac rods in a triangular foundation, sewn with fine splints of willow or, less frequently, sumac or cottonwood. The stiff narrow coils created a corrugated surface.

Unidentified girl posing in basket at the Alvarado Hotel, Albuquerque, New Mexico, ca. 1920s. Photo Archives, Museum of New Mexico.

Decoration was done with black splints of devil's claw and occasional segments of red yucca root. The tough devil's claw was generally used for the center of the basket and also for the plain lashed rims. Very rarely red or blue-green dyed splints were used in the designs.

The most common baskets were shallow bowl-trays in a wide range of sizes, from six inches in diameter to thirty-six inches. Designs were generally symmetrical and centripetal with radiating lines of triangles, zigzags, petals, or points (fig. 116). Some patterns were interlocked and others were concentric or circular, but the most interesting were those that included silhouette figures of humans as well as dogs, horses, and other animals (fig. 117). Deep bowls with straight sides (fig. 130) were uncommon, but *ollas* of various sizes and proportions were hallmarks of Western Apache basketry. Occasional tall slender *ollas* reached a height of more than four feet, and many were made that were between twenty-four and thirty-six inches high (fig. 133). Broad *ollas* with marked shoulders (fig. 132), *ollas* with flaring necks, and *ollas* with nearly globular bodies were decorated with the same designs. Some were covered with rectangular figures, some with allover netted designs of diamonds, others were encircled with zigzag or checkered bands, and many incorporated the life figures used on the coiled trays (fig. 133). The native use of these vase-shaped baskets is uncertain. Although most of them were produced for the market, ollas were also made by these Apaches during the 1880s and some of them served to hold corn and other foods.

It is a sad fact that these fine baskets were no longer being made by 1975. In the 1980s a small group of four or five women were attempting to revive the art, but their expertise was slow to develop and their small coiled baskets were poor imitations of the great baskets produced by their grandmothers. Twined basket making, on the other hand, was thriving and expanding in the 1980s, possibly because the traditional twined burden baskets were for many years important elements in the young women's Sunrise Ceremony in which they were initiated into Apache society. The classic burden baskets were twined with willow or mulberry splints over whole rod warps, reinforced with two heavy juniper U-shaped rods, and finished with double rims: the upper rim was made with heavy galvanized wire for many years and the lower rim of a bundle that included the upper ends of the warps with some added splints. The two rims were wrapped with strips of buckskin (fig. 145). Typically the burden baskets were decorated with narrow vertical panels of buckskin with long slender depending fringes. The bases were usually covered with buckskin and/or cloth, which was edged with additional fringe. Further decoration usually consist-

ed of several encircling bands of checks or triangles in red, black, and, occasionally, blue or green (fig. 170). Some of the colored designs were dyed splints, others were painted on the exterior of the basket, stitch by stitch. Although the baskets were usually plain twined to produce vertical parallel corrugations, textural changes were sometimes introduced with bands of twill twining, and three-strand twining was frequently used for extra strength below the rim and near the bottom.

These elaborately constructed and decorated burden baskets were used primarily for carrying the family's personal effects when moving from one camp to another. Other baskets were used for gathering and transporting foods such as corn, mescal, seeds, and roots. These carrying baskets were the same shape and size as the first type, but they were less rigid because they were made without the U-shaped reinforcing rods. They also lacked the buckskin fringes and were decorated simply with two or three bands of checks or diagonal lines. Because they required less work than the other baskets they could be more easily replaced when they were broken or worn out from the hard use they received, as Grenville Goodwin remarked in Ferg and Kessel, 1987.

Twining also was used to make water bottles and jars of many shapes and sizes. These usually were twined with mulberry splints and liberally coated with piñon pitch inside and outside (fig. 174). Before coating they were often rubbed with a mash of crushed juniper leaves or even goat dung and then covered with red ochre, which usually showed through the pitch. One special type of bottle was a double-bodied or dumbbell shape that was designed to be carried on the hip with a strap over one shoulder. Most water bottles have loops of horsehair or bent twigs for attaching the carrying straps.

Although few of them are used now, many water bottles are still made, especially by the Cibecue Apaches of the San Carlos Reservation in eastern Arizona. In New Mexico, several women make twined burden baskets of mulberry, but many more twined baskets are produced at San Carlos. Led by matriarch Cecilia Henry, the daughters and daughters-in-law of her family have made basketry an important craft on their reservation. Large conical baskets twined with willow are decorated with half-twist designs of checked or ticked bands and figures of eagles and antlered deer. They are decked with commercial leather fringe, which is usually terminated with tin cones, and range in size from very large (three feet in height and diameter) to baskets half an inch high that are sold as earrings. Whether or not they are traditional in shape and function is less important than their role in keeping basket making alive and healthy among the Western Apaches.

Havasupai woman with carrying basket and water basket, ca. 1920. Early Western Apaches, as well as contemporary, use these conical baskets. Photo Archives, Museum of New Mexico.

PREHISTORIC POTTERY OF NEW MEXICO

STEWART PECKHAM

Anasazi Kiva, Jemez River Canyon in north-central New Mexico.
Photograph by Paul Logsdon.

POTTERY MAKING IS THE BEST KNOWN and most enduring craft of the Pueblo Indians of the Southwest. Pueblo pottery has earned for itself and its makers the interest and respect of specialists in the fields of archaeology, ethnology, art history, and museology around the world. Millions of pottery vessels have been fashioned by Pueblo potters in the years since the craft was introduced from Mexico, but relatively few of these are on view in museums. Many are housed in private collections, and many more have been destroyed or disappeared.

Pueblo pottery served countless daily household functions: jars, bowls, and dippers were used for storing, cooking, and serving food, carrying and storing water, and even storing personal belongings. Special pottery items such as prayermeal bowls, ritual canteens, pipes, figurines, and effigy vessels were used for religious purposes. Pots also were traded or presented as gifts to both distant and nearby groups. Even after they were broken, recycled fragments were reworked into pottery-making tools, scoops, gaming pieces, pendants, "chinking stones" in masonry con-

Prehistoric pots (900–pre-1300) excavated at the ancient settlement
of Pueblo Bonito, Chaco Canyon, New Mexico. Photo Archives,
Museum of New Mexico.

struction, and pulverized to mix with, or temper, clay for new pots.

Whole pots and fragments of prehistoric pottery probably have preoccupied southwestern archaeologists longer and led to more knowledge about the human condition in the ancient Southwest then any other type of artifact. Pottery making is influenced by regional differences in raw materials, technology, and aesthetics, and thus it frequently helps to establish a framework on which the principal prehistoric cultures and their branches may be reconstructed. Classified into innumerable *wares* and *types,* pottery becomes an invaluable tool for dating prehistoric sites, tracing the development of art styles, following routes of interregional trade, and validating the continuity of one of the most ancient and valued traditions of today's Pueblo Indians.

We know that pottery did not develop on this continent in the Southwest. It originated perhaps as early as 2500 B.C. in southern Mexico, or even farther south, taking twenty-seven centuries to spread northward throughout Mexico, from tribe to tribe and settlement to settlement, until its technology ultimately was transmitted to the Southwest Indians. Actually, pottery technology may have reached the Southwest at various times by several different routes: up the west coast of Mexico into southwestern Arizona, up the Rio Grande into the vicinity of El Paso, Texas. However, the Pueblo pottery tradition seems to have followed the flanks of the Sierra Madre Occidental, the great mountain chain that stretches from lower Mexico northward into the southern Southwest. Current estimates place its initiation in the Southwest at A.D. 200.

At that time, and for the previous eight thousand years, a group of Indians (the Cochise culture) lived and hunted and gathered foods in the mountains, valleys, and desert around the panhandle of southwestern New Mexico and adjacent parts of southeastern Arizona and northern Mexico. For these early Indian groups, life probably was short and seemingly unvarying from generation to generation. If we can judge by contemporary Pueblo attitudes, time was not a matter of much concern in Cochise Cul-

ture. The past was regarded as unimportant: the present time and place were what mattered. However, over time subtle and significant changes may be distinguished in Cochise sites: locations of campsites were shifted and stone and bone tools evolved into more effective forms. The people began to explore the land and learn more about the resources available to them as they adapted to an increasingly arid environment.

The most significant change to visit the Cochise people involved the shift to agriculture, when the cultivation of maize, squash, and beans was introduced to them by Mexican Indians. Archaeologists differ on when agriculture was introduced in the Southwest, varying in their estimates between 6000 and 1000 B.C. or 200 and 300 B.C. Unquestionably it was a revolutionary development although a slow one, enabling the Cochise people to vary and improve their wild game and plant food diet with domesticated plant foods and, even more important, to store crops for later use.

For thousands of years the Cochise people had gathered, stored, and served food in well-woven, portable, lightweight baskets or cached food and belongings in underground storage pits. This pattern certainly continued, but following the introduction of agriculture the more durable and protective qualities of pottery containers must have been especially appreciated.

THE MOGOLLON POTTERY TRADITION

The Cochise people and other prepottery cultures of the Southwest may have observed their southern neighbors' pottery making before they actually learned all the techniques of its manufacture. In various parts of the Southwest, archaeologists have found fragments of rough, thick, poorly fired clay bowls held together with binders of shredded juniper bark or other plant fiber and usually bearing impressions of coiled basketry into which flattened coils or strips of clay had been pressed. This "pseudo-pottery" may have been an attempt to replicate the true pottery that southwestern hunting and gathering Indians had seen during forays into what is now Mexico.

Most prehistoric pottery in the New World was made using a technique known as coiling. Vessel walls were constructed of bands or ropes of clay laid one on top of another and pinched together to build a pot to the desired size and form. Throwing a pot on a potter's wheel is an Old World development that appears not to have been accepted by New World potters. Even today, Pueblo potters prefer and perpetuate the coiling tradition with which they skillfully produce bowls and jars of exceptional symmetry. The fact that the pseudo-pottery often was constructed of coils or strips of clay may show that prepottery southwestern Indians had at least some familiarity with coiling as a pottery-making technique, or that they were adapting the techniques of coiled basketry to their work in clay. A third possibility is that the unfired clay vessels may simply have been purposefully made to line baskets used for parching or toasting seeds. As late as the nineteenth century, some Indian groups in the western United States parched seeds by swirling them around with hot coals in baskets to make them more digestible. The Cochise people may have done likewise, possibly using a clay basket liner to prevent the red-hot coals from damaging their baskets or to prolong the lives of worn-out ones.

The Museum of New Mexico excavation of a Mogollon Culture site in a woodland area not far from Quemado in west-central New Mexico yielded a significant find. Quemado, a Spanish term often referring to an area burned by a forest fire, is appropriate, since the site included a semisubterranean dwelling, or pit house, that may have been destroyed during a forest fire. When the pit house burned, its occupants were forced to abandon it in great haste, leaving behind a treasure trove of hundreds of utensils and personal belongings: stone and bone tools and carbonized remains of foodstuffs, sandals, hair and plant fiber cordage, and fourteen pottery vessels. Tree-ring dating of charred roof timbers shows that the pit house had been built about A.D. 487 and suggests that its burning occurred a few years later.

Pottery found at this site was technologically more developed and represents very early examples of what is called Mogollon Brownware. The rocks (basalt and tuff), mountains, and mesas of southwestern New Mexico were formed by vulcanism, and subsequent breakdown of some of these iron-rich deposits produced clay. Potters fired this clay at a relatively low temperature in the presence of oxygen (an oxidizing atmosphere) to produce a gray-brown to reddish-brown pottery.

No longer simple camps, the early Mogollon sites have an air of permanence about them. Generally situated on upland wooded areas overlooking potentially good agricultural areas along principal drainages, these sites are often recognized by a greater frequency and variety of pottery and other artifacts on their surfaces and by shallow depressions marking the locations of formal dwellings such as pit houses. The later sites are marked by mounds of rubble.

Whole or restorable pottery vessels from early Mogollon sites show that useful basketry shapes—bowls, globular jars, shallow trays, and bottle-like forms—were sometimes copied in pottery. New forms also were developed as Mogollon potters became increasingly sophisticated in their craft. The surfaces of graceful shapes, such as the Alma Plain olla, or water jar (fig. 6), were polished with smooth stream pebbles.

For the next one thousand years, Mogollon potters experimented with and perfected texturing of vessel exteriors, first by scoring, incising, or leaving some coils unobliterated around jar necks, and later with an almost infinite variety of manipulations of the coils to produce what is called "corrugated" ware. Archaeologists generally consider such textured pottery as utility or culinary ware used primarily for cooking or storage.

Almost as soon as pottery was introduced, Mogollon potters learned slipping, the application of a fine-grained, usually red-firing clay that would cover imperfections of vessel surfaces and accept a better polish. Though rarely occurring in quantity, this redware may have been an intermediate stage in the development of both the painted pottery and smudged ware

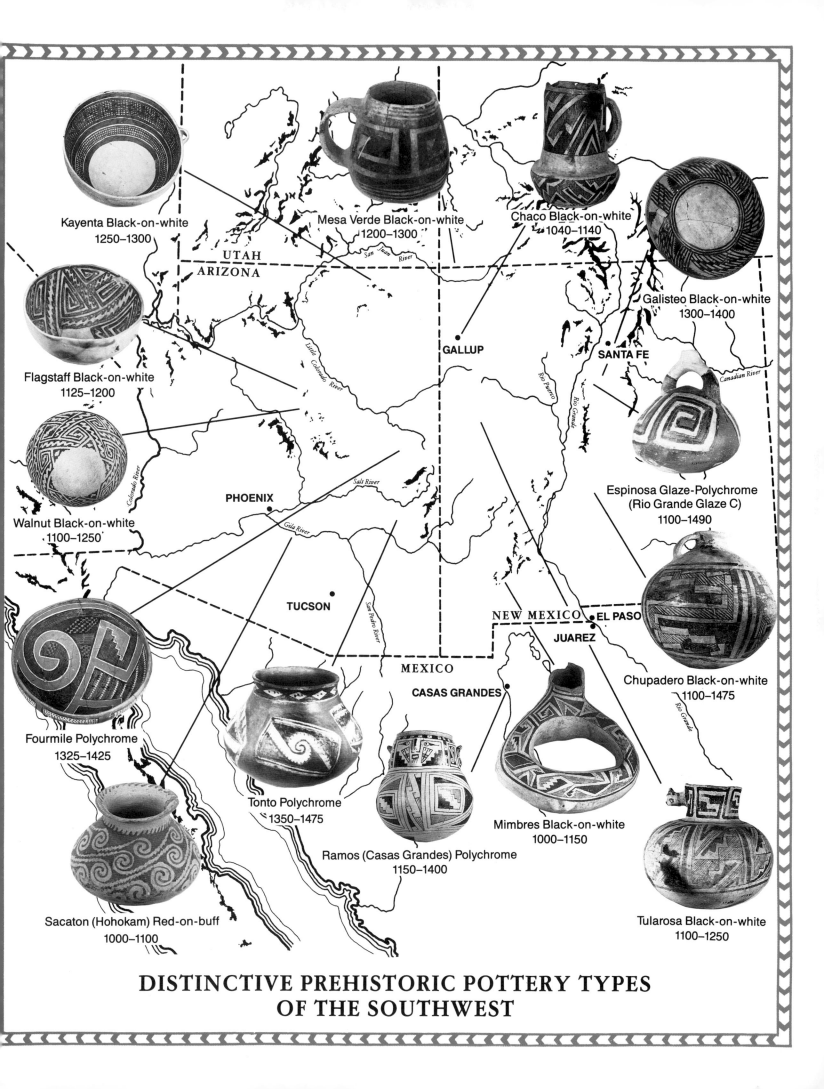

Kayenta Black-on-white
1250–1300

Mesa Verde Black-on-white
1200–1300

Chaco Black-on-white
1040–1140

Galisteo Black-on-white
1300–1400

Flagstaff Black-on-white
1125–1200

Walnut Black-on-white
1100–1250

Espinosa Glaze-Polychrome
(Rio Grande Glaze C)
1100–1490

Chupadero Black-on-white
1100–1475

Fourmile Polychrome
1325–1425

Tonto Polychrome
1350–1475

Ramos (Casas Grandes) Polychrome
1150–1400

Mimbres Black-on-white
1000–1150

Sacaton (Hohokam) Red-on-buff
1000–1100

Tularosa Black-on-white
1100–1250

UTAH
ARIZONA

San Juan River

GALLUP

SANTA FE

Canadian River

Little Colorado River

Rio Puerco

Rio Grande

Colorado River

Salt River

PHOENIX

Gila River

TUCSON

San Pedro River

NEW MEXICO   EL PASO

JUAREZ

MEXICO

CASAS GRANDES

Rio Grande

DISTINCTIVE PREHISTORIC POTTERY TYPES
OF THE SOUTHWEST

commonly found in food bowl forms.

It could have been the influence from northern Mexico, or from the Hohokam Culture in southern Arizona, that, by about A.D. 650, led Mogollon potters in southwestern New Mexico to apply simple, linear, red decoration to tan-slipped bowl interiors. Within a century, slip color had changed to white, and by A.D. 800 black-firing mineral pigment was used for bold, largely geometric painted decoration—so-called Mangas (or Mimbres Bold Face) Black-on-white (fig. 11). These designs sometimes shared a decorative style with Anasazi Culture pottery found in the northern Southwest and in the Hohokam area in southern Arizona (fig. 10).

By A.D. 1000, the bold designs had given way to one of the most distinctive southwestern pottery types, Mimbres Black-on-white (figs. 26, 28, 30). Nowhere else in the Southwest would prehistoric potters achieve such artistic mastery as in the precisely drawn and almost photographic accuracy of this pottery type. Art historian J. J. Brody likens the creamy white background of Mimbres Black-on-white to an artist's canvas on which Mimbres potters painted detailed portraits of animals (fig. 20), birds, insects (fig. 29), daily life, ritual, mythical figures (fig. 21), and the Indians themselves (fig. 22), any of which might be worked into a geometric design as well. Bowl exteriors apparently were considered of lesser importance and usually were not slipped. The type occurs primarily in bowl forms, though some jars and effigies are known. Most commonly, the bowls have been found as "grave goods" with human burials, though many vessels show evidence of wear from frequent household use. A hole was punched in the bottom of the bowls found at burial sites or they were purposefully broken. This usually has been interpreted as a ritual "killing" of the bowl so its spirit might be freed to go with that of the person with whom it was buried.

Classic Mimbres Black-on-white has been much sought by museums and, regrettably, private collectors. The greater resources of the latter have led to inflated values for the pottery, which has encouraged professional looters to use bulldozers on Mimbres ruins in their search for pottery vessels. The result has been the total destruction of many prehistoric cultural remains in the Mimbres Province and the loss of untold amounts of information about one of New Mexico's —and the nation's—most creative prehistoric Indian groups.

Smudging—the intentional smoke-blackening of highly burnished (and possibly slipped) vessel interiors—began about A.D. 600 and persisted as long as the Mogollon Culture in New Mexico (A.D. 1300 to 1350), and perhaps even later in some areas. A technique commonly employed by most Mogollon potters, particularly where painted pottery was not produced in quantity, smudging is found mainly on textured vessels, the utility bowls that appear to have served almost exclusively for holding food. Although similar to modern Pueblo Indian "black-on-black" pottery of the middle Rio Grande and Tewa Basin provinces, Mogollon smudged pottery appears to have been produced by a firing process that drives carbon into the interior surface of the vessel. Modern blackware is largely produced by reduction firing when the burning fuel is smothered with powdered animal dung.

Probably as a result of a severe drought in southwestern New Mexico in the 1130s and 1150s, the makers of Mimbres Black-on-white abandoned their homeland by about A.D. 1150. Some of the tribal character was maintained by those who moved eastward into the lower Rio Grande and beyond, ultimately settling in the Tularosa Basin near Alamogordo, New Mexico. By the 1200s, however, the Mimbres pottery tradition had become extinct, lost in the culture of the Jornada Province of the Mogollon Culture.

North of the Mimbres Province, in the general vicinities of Reserve and Quemado, New Mexico, potters of the Cibola Province of the Mogollon followed much the same evolutionary path as did Mimbres potters. It is possible, though, that people in the southern part of the Cibola Province made little or no painted pottery of their own, preferring to obtain by trade whatever they needed from the Mimbres Province, at least until the early 1000s. However, classic

Mimbres Bowls, 1000–1150, excavated at ancient sites in
southwestern New Mexico and showing "kill" holes.
Photograph by Douglas Kahn.

Mimbres Black-on-white is rare in later southern Cibola Province sites, suggesting that Indians of the two provinces drew away from one another in the early 1000s and maintained virtually no contact after A.D. 1100. Painted pottery, such as the Tularosa Black-on-white bird effigy (fig. 24) (possibly a ceremonial container), probably was obtained from potters in the northern part of the Cibola Province. Southern Cibola people used finely polished, smudged, almost iridescent Tularosa Fillet Rim as food serving bowls.

THE ANASAZI CULTURE

Even as Mogollon potters gained proficiency in pottery making, knowledge of the craft continued to spread rapidly, and by A.D. 500 it had reached other hunting and gathering Indians of the Oshara Tradition as far north as northwestern New Mexico and southwestern Colorado. By A.D. 700, pottery was being made in many parts of northern Arizona, southern Utah, and east into the Rio Grande Valley. How-

Archaeologist removes paper-thin fragments of undecorated layer of
plaster from kiva wall at the Pueblo III-IV site at Pottery Mound,
New Mexico, 1954–1962. At right, uncovering kiva mural to
expose prehistoric geometric design. Photos courtesy
Laboratory of Anthropology.

ever, in most of these latter areas the pottery was gray rather than brown.

Beginning not far north of U.S. Highway 60 in New Mexico and a line extending westward into Arizona along the edge of the Mogollon Rim, sources and composition of pottery clays changed markedly. North of this line, instead of the residual clays of volcanic deposits of the rugged mountains and valleys of the Mogollon area, early potters found sedimentary clays that outcrop on the mesas and prairies of the Colorado Plateau. Formed in shallow Cretaceous seas over sixty million years ago, these clays

are low in iron and rich in carbonaceous material and produce pottery that usually fires to a gray, white, or buff color. The grayish color provides archaeologists with a major distinction between the brownware-producing Mogollon Culture in the south and the grayware of the Anasazi Culture in the northern Southwest. However, there is more to this distinction than the amount of iron in the clay. Anasazi potters developed a firing method that first allowed air (oxygen) to reach the clay (oxidation) and burn out the carbon, and then excluded air (reduction) to convert iron oxides present to lower orders, producing a lighter

Student archaeologists at Pueblo III–IV site at Pottery Mound
uncover the floor of the painted kiva. Artist's rendering of kiva
mural is visible at left. Photograph courtesy
Laboratory of Anthropology.

gray final color.

Though basic gray predominated, archaeologists recognize regional differences in the wares based on the specific tempering material added to the clay to reduce shrinkage during initial drying and firing. In most provinces, rather coarse, rounded sand or crushed sandstone was added as temper, though in much of the Chuska and Mesa Verde provinces, crushed volcanic rock was used. Still, shrinkage occurred, sometimes causing the temper to protrude slightly, producing rough vessel surfaces, characteristically so in the type Lino Gray (fig. 8).

As in the Mogollon area, grayware culinary or utility pottery went through a sequence of surface textures, though generally not as varied. Nor did the Anasazi practice smudging. Earliest Anasazi potters commonly embellished vessel exteriors with a coating or slip of red pigment, made of hematite, applied after firing. This may have been an Anasazi attempt to replicate the permanent fired-on red slips found on contemporary Mogollon pottery that was occasionally traded north to the Anasazi. The difference, of course, was that the Anasazi red slip was essentially a watercolor which would easily wash off, often leav-

Excavation at Pueblo Bonito, Chaco Canyon, New Mexico,
ca. 1895. Photo Archives, Museum of New Mexico.

ing only a faint rosy hue on the vessel exterior. Because of the elusiveness of this paint, archaeologists refer to it as "fugitive red."

By about A.D. 600, if not somewhat earlier, Anasazi potters had begun painting some of their pottery. As with clays and tempers, they had a choice. Potters in the Upper San Juan Province used a vegetal or carbon pigment made from the residue of boiled-down leaves and stems of the Rocky Mountain Bee Plant *(Cleome serrulata)*; Anasazi in northeastern Arizona preferred Tansy Mustard *(Descurainia richardsonii)*. In most eastern Anasazi provinces, though, an iron oxide was ground up and sometimes mixed with the

plant pigment. Whether a "carbon" paint or an "iron" paint, the color intended was usually black, though iron paint often fires to a brownish black.

At first, painted decoration was simply applied to the rough surface of the vessel. By about A.D. 800, Anasazi potters had found that by applying a slip or coating of very fine grained, white-firing clay to vessel surfaces, it became possible to cover up the roughness and base color and polish it to achieve a more appealing contrasting background for the painted decoration.

Early Anasazi potters appear to have painted designs copied from the woven, almost free-form and randomly placed designs of their basketry, but by A.D. 850 or 900 the range of Anasazi pottery decoration had become restricted to geometric figures—triangles, parallel lines, scrolls (fig. 14)—and, a little later, broad-line solids and hatch-filled elements (fig. 27). Whether it was purely a matter of potter's preference or a conservative mandate is uncertain, but the range of painted design appears to have become more limited. From the beginning of pottery painting until about A.D. 1150, painted decoration was almost exclusively applied to the concave, interior surface of bowls and the convex, outside surface of jars and pitchers.

With the introduction of painted decoration and the fuller appreciation of the versatility of pottery, potters began to use different kinds of temper and clay mixtures and different surface treatments depending on the proposed function of a pot. Painted vessels, usually bowls, pitchers, canteens, and dippers, held or served food or water. Many unpainted, rough-surfaced vessels—often, but not always, large jars—were used for storing foods and cooking. Pots found with their exteriors encrusted with soot obviously had been used for cooking. (Painted vessels almost never show such use.)

Styles of culinary vessels changed much more slowly than those of painted pots, and most decoration involved changing the exterior texture of the coils of clay as the culinary pot was being made. Occasionally the earliest culinary pottery bore simple incised decoration around the neck. By about A.D. 800, potters were leaving broad coils visible around the necks of jars (fig. 9). Later, these coils became increasingly narrow, ultimately resembling the undulating surface of corrugated cardboard or roofing material. By A.D. 950 these corrugations were being manipulated with the fingers to produce exuberant, carefully aligned, and patterned indentations.

Even before A.D. 1000, the fashion of making and aligning the bold indented corrugations led to making the precise indentations smaller and smaller (fig. 19). However, for some reason by A.D. 1075 the potters apparently were less interested in making aesthetically pleasing culinary pottery. Some archaeologists feel that the Anasazi ability at about this time

to produce food surpluses required the production of more storage vessels, and this demand led to increasing carelessness in finishing storage jar exteriors. This process went through several additional stages during the next five hundred years, leading to the coils becoming increasingly obliterated until, by A.D. 1600, when Spanish conquistadores settled in New Mexico, culinary pottery was again rough or only slightly smoothed, very much as it had been when pottery was first introduced.

THE PUERCO–SAN JUAN POTTERY TRADITIONS

Probably no other archaeological locality in North America has proved to be so enigmatic to archaeologists as Chaco Canyon. Along a scant dozen miles of an entrenched arroyo, in one of the most desolate parts of northwestern New Mexico, lie thirteen huge masonry ruins and hundreds of lesser ones. Until about A.D. 850 or 900, the Anasazi who lived there seem to have lived like any of their contemporaries: individual families occupying dispersed dwellings of fifteen to twenty rooms, farming, making pottery, and probably practicing a religion promoting rain making, good crops and good hunting, individual cures, and general well-being.

Around A.D. 919, as suggested by tree-ring dating, a group of people on the north side of the canyon began to remodel their dwelling, adding about twenty-five new and larger rooms. It may not have been the precise event that started the florescence of Chaco Canyon, but it seems to have been the beginning of the growth of the huge structure we know today as Pueblo Bonito. Intermittently until about A.D. 1130, it and other settlements, like Chetro Ketl, Peñasco Blanco, Una Vida, and Hungo Pavi, experienced spurts of building, using architectural techniques and features generally unparalleled on the south side of Chaco Canyon or elsewhere.

The magnitude of the buildings was matched by the numbers and increased size of ceremonial chambers (kivas) and their accoutrements and, eventually,

Aeriel view of Pueblo Bonito at Chaco Canyon.
Photo Archives, Museum of New Mexico.

by their association with more elaborate artifacts. Among archaeologists, there is no real consensus on what brought about these developments, but there seems little doubt that the cluster of buildings was constructed for some special purpose.

Archaeologists have hypothesized many explanations for the unique character of Chaco Canyon: at Chaco there flourished a trading system instigated by affluent Indian entrepreneurs from Mexico; it was the hub of a network of roads reaching to all parts of the eastern Anasazi area; it incorporated a long-distance communications center involving signal towers and was a center for seasonal religious observances. Furthermore, Chaco was the focus of an integrated public works program that built great religious structures as well as storehouses as part of the distributional center of a prehistoric welfare program that channeled food surpluses from some Anasazi areas to other less fortunate Anasazi groups whose food supplies suffered from periodic drought. The impetus for the un-

matched growth of Chaco Canyon may never be identified in the archaeological record.

At each of these new and exceptionally large buildings at Chaco Canyon, initial expansion seems to have coincided with the beginning manufacture of a distinctive type of pottery—Red Mesa Black-on-white (fig. 14). Almost coincidentally, the Red Mesa style of decoration appears on pottery throughout Anasazi and Mogollon provinces, as if all were responding to the same stimulus. The style remained popular for 150 to 200 years, but it was gradually supplanted by four partly contemporary types: Gallup Black-on-white (fig. 18), Escavada Black-on-white, Chaco Black-on-white, and Socorro Black-on-white, some of which were made in different parts of the San Juan Basin.

For more than two hundred years, construction of the great towns at Chaco Canyon continued, but by A.D. 1130 new construction ceased and what appears to be Chaco influence on architecture and pottery making throughout the San Juan Basin came to an end. The nemesis of the Anasazi—drought—caused the lowering of the Chaco River to the point that its periodic flow could no longer be drawn upon for agriculture, forcing the abandonment of many of the great villages. With this drastic change came shifts in pottery making: iron oxide paint ceased to be used by those who remained in the Chaco Province. Instead, potters adopted carbon, or vegetal, paint and some of the decorative styles used by potters in the Chuska Province, some thirty-six miles to the west, and the Mesa Verde Province seventy-two miles north, producing the type known as Chaco-McElmo Black-on-white (fig. 23). The latter two provinces continued to prosper while Chaco declined, and Mesa Verde Black-on-white, with its thick, highly polished slip and carefully drawn designs (sometimes on the exteriors of bowls), was produced by the inhabitants of the spectacular cliff-dwellings at Mesa Verde and the large villages along the San Juan River near Farmington.

Finally, a prolonged drought (A.D. 1276 to 1299) dealt the death blow to the Anasazi of the San Juan Basin. Combined disasters—repeated crop failures, drying up of springs, exhaustion of emergency food supplies, and, probably, both physical and mental deterioration—forced them to abandon the region entirely by the early 1300s. Survivors migrated to new homes in provinces in all directions but north, with the Rio Grande provinces probably receiving the greatest influx of settlers. The migrants carried with them what they could, but most pottery was left behind. As they moved into areas with long-established cultural preferences as well as unfamiliar natural resources, most Mesa Verde migrants gave up—or forgot—their old pottery-making traditions, often adopting those of their host provinces. In subsequent centuries, information about their San Juan Basin homeland also was lost until it was rediscovered through the labors of archaeologists.

THE UPPER SAN JUAN-GALLINA TRADITION

A different situation seems to have prevailed along the Upper San Juan River drainage some forty miles east and northeast of the modern city of Farmington. As early as A.D. 300, farming Indians in the Upper San Juan Province were living in small villages of permanent spacious dome-shaped surface dwellings, and by A.D. 500 they appear to have been at least somewhat familiar with pottery making, mainly of small vessels, effigies, and pipes, thereby meeting the archaeologist's three basic criteria for the Anasazi Culture. The early pottery was a brownware resulting from oxidation firing, leading some archaeologists to postulate Mogollon Culture influence (though over 150 miles of Anasazi terrain lies between the Upper San Juan and the nearest Mogollon provinces).

During the next two hundred to three hundred years Upper San Juan developments in architecture and especially pottery were far outpaced by their Mesa Verde neighbors to the west and Chaco and Chuska Anasazi to the southwest. Not until the late 700s and early 800s did Upper San Juan potters begin making larger, more functional jars and bowls of grayware. Nevertheless, for the next 250 years their ceramic creativity seems to have focused on sometimes graceful and innovative plain gray vessel forms. Little interest was shown in painted pottery, an exception being a pictorial Piedra Black-on-white bowl (a unique decorative treatment on any Anasazi pottery), which shows bird tracks leading to a hunting net. Presumably the bird was caught and then served in the bowl. Even more unusual is a Bancos Black-on-white effigy of a fish, one of two recovered by the Museum of New Mexico at Sambrito Village, an extensive pit house site in the Navajo Reservoir District just south of the New Mexico–Colorado boundary. Its significance is not known; fish may have been an important food source along the Upper San Juan River. It would appear that the peripheral location of the Upper San Juan Province relative to the rest of the Anasazi Culture and the degradation of its environment combined to slow its cultural development, so much so that by A.D. 1050 much of the province was abandoned.

At least one group from the Upper San Juan moved southeastward to the general vicinity of Cuba,

New Mexico, where it was recognized in the 1200s as the Gallina Province, or, as it is sometimes called, the Largo-Gallina Phase. It is characterized by habitation sites commonly established in defensible locations; massive-walled dwellings, both subterranean and at ground level; occasional towers that may have been defensive or used for storage or for signalling; religious practices that did not employ formal structures recognizable as kivas; apparent, and possibly late, preoccupation with warfare; and little evidence of peaceful contacts with other Anasazi groups. In short, the group did not display many traits regarded as typically Anasazi.

Isolation from their neighbors and an unfriendly natural environment made only slight contributions to Gallina advancement. Even in the 1200s, Gallina potters appear to have been inexpert. Evidence suggests that they were not inclined to follow the trends initiated by potters in western New Mexico, such as care in vessel forming, application of thick, well-polished slips, and development of intricate and aesthetically pleasing painted decoration. The simple quartered layout of the carbon painted Gallina Black-on-white food bowl, albeit with dot-filling, seems to reflect their conservatism if not lack of imagination. Possibly these potters had more pressing matters to worry about.

The Gallina Black-on-white effigy of a horned toad is unique among people hitherto not known for making pottery effigies and also because it shows at least selective Gallina concern for decorative detail on pottery. To us, the horned toad is almost invisible as it blends in with dry grass and soil, but to the Gallina potter, familiar with the land and its fauna and the horned toad's importance as a conspicuous survivor in the desert, its representation may have expressed a prayer for similar survival by its maker.

THE WESTERN PUEBLO TRADITION

During the late 1000s and early 1100s in the Upper Little Colorado region of west-central New Mexico and just across the border in Arizona, Anasazi potters developed a thick, well-polished red slip that became the background color for much of their painted pottery. With eastern Anasazi and Mogollon potters producing rather bland white, gray, or brown pottery, it is not surprising that the showy White Mountain Redware was widely traded in both Anasazi and Mogollon provinces. Notable in this regard was Wingate Black-on-red (fig. 17), which had begun to reach the Chaco Canyon Province in the late 1100s and was still popular in the Rio Grande provinces in the 1200s. Its successor, St. Johns Polychrome (fig. 25), with compact black interior designs on a red-orange slip and simpler white decoration on orange on the exterior, was widely traded in the 1200s and early 1300s, even as far as the Taos-Picuris Province in the northern Rio Grande. Some St. Johns Polychrome and later types show evidence that their makers were experimenting with different pigments and firing techniques, sometimes achieving a semiglaze quality on painted decoration. By the early 1300s, they were consistently using a black copper-manganese glaze decoration on a red or white background.

Black-on-white pottery continued to be made in east-central Arizona and adjacent New Mexico and was contemporary with St. Johns Polychrome (A.D. 1175 to 1300). The "stirrup canteen" of Klageto Black-on-white (fig. 37) seems out of place in the Southwest, but the form occurs as early as the 700s in southwestern Colorado and was made as recently as the 1300s in the middle Rio Grande Province in New Mexico. Similar examples of the form have been found as far south as Peru.

MERGING TRADITIONS

By the late 1200s, the entire San Juan Basin had been abandoned, and many of its former inhabitants had moved southeast toward the better-watered areas of the Rio Grande and Acoma provinces and probably to the Zuni and Hopi areas. Where the migrants went after they left the San Juan Basin is still undetermined.

Abandonment of their homes, together with the

Gallina Black-on-white effigy, 1200–1275.
Photograph by Douglas Kahn.

ordeals of migration (including attempts to move into areas already occupied by other groups) constituted major disasters for the San Juan Anasazi. They and their ancestors had lived for centuries in close association with one another. They had accumulated a vast knowledge of the available resources of the Basin and knew how to use them to best advantage. By the late 1200s they were on the move, sometimes stopping to try out a new area for settlement and then moving on. Wherever they went they had to adjust to new terrain, searching out reliable water, usable plants, and other natural resources, building new homes, and establishing contact with hundreds of other Anasazi, perhaps many of them strangers, who were in the same situation.

Accustomed to building masonry dwellings in the San Juan Basin, the migrants found few places in the Rio Grande region that provided stone suitable for such construction. Similarly, the available raw materials for pottery making were unfamiliar and probably not as well adapted to this use as had been those they were accustomed to in the San Juan Basin. In many areas it seems as if they adopted the pottery-making practices of those already in residence in the Rio Grande region. This meant forgetting some of the old ways in favor of new ones. There was continuity of the pottery-making tradition in general, but the merging of numerous traditions often led to the production of pottery that only occasionally resembled what they had made before.

POTTERY OF THE PROTOHISTORIC

By A.D. 1350 to 1400, Anasazi migrations to new homelands in the Rio Grande drainage had ended as the populations concentrated in the Pajarito Plateau near Los Alamos; the Galisteo Basin and Pecos provinces south of Santa Fe; the Chama Valley northwest of Española; the Tesuque-Nambé drainage north of Santa Fe; the Jemez district northwest of Albuquerque; the middle Rio Grande, from Cochiti Pueblo south to near Belen; and the Salinas Province southeast of Albuquerque. Subsequently, the Anasazi consolidated their holdings by joining previously separate pueblos into larger ones. Though the traumatic disruption of Anasazi life had ended, much of the fourteenth century seems to have been devoted to adjusting to new surroundings, and throughout the fourteenth and fifteenth centuries they were increasingly preoccupied with warfare.

Pottery of the first half of the Protohistoric Period (A.D. 1300 to 1500) in the Rio Grande region quickly differentiated into two main groups: glaze-decorated (in the Middle Rio Grande, Rio Abajo, Galisteo Basin, Pecos, and Salinas provinces) and carbon-painted (in the more northerly Taos-Picuris, Tewa Basin, Pajarito Plateau, and Jemez provinces). Glaze-decorated pottery was produced or extensively used by most of the prehistoric pueblos south of Santa Fe, primarily by the ancestors of the modern Keres and southern Tiwa pueblos. Archaeologists distinguish a series of glaze-decorated pottery groups (A through F) based on the gradual changes in the shape of the rims of bowls.

Some of the first glaze pottery types were polychromes (more than two colors—usually the black glaze on red and white, pink, or buff background), apparently due to influence from the Zuni Pueblo area, where glaze-decorated pottery originated. Except for the earliest types, designs are typically bold and show little similarity to the pottery the Rio Grande Anasazi made when they still lived in the San Juan Basin. The glaze pigments appear to have come almost exclusively from the Cerrillos Mining District south of Santa Fe, where lead ore, turquoise, and other minerals occur in abundance. There, the prehistoric Indians used massive stone hammers and picks to mine the narrow veins of lead ore that crop out on the surface of the ground. Glaze-decorated pottery was traded widely, especially to Plains Indians. Potsherds of glazeware have been found on sites as far away as east-central Texas.

Best known of the carbon-painted pottery types is the so-called Biscuitware of the Tewa Basin Province, so named because its early types resemble the soft porous stage of modern commercially made glazed pottery. Decorated with carbon paint, this Biscuitware is divided into three main types: Abiquiu Black-on-gray, or Biscuit A (A.D. 1375 to 1425); Bandelier

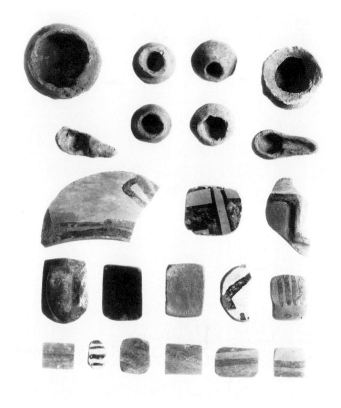

Prehistoric potsherds excavated at Unshagi ruin in the Jemez Mountains of New Mexico.

Black-on-gray, or Biscuit B (A.D. 1425 to 1475) (fig. 31); and Cuyamungue Black-on-tan, or Biscuit C (A.D. 1475 to 1600). A fourth type, Tsankawi Black-on-cream (A.D. 1550 to 1650) bridges the gap between the Prehistoric (before the establishment, in 1598, of the Spanish colony in New Mexico) and the Early Historic Periods (when the Pueblo Indians came increasingly under Spanish domination and influence). Typically, the Biscuitwares were made by the prehistoric ancestors of the modern Tewa pueblos located north and northwest of Santa Fe. One of the most distinctive design elements of the Biscuitwares is the Awanyu figure, an angled or curved line or panel with a serrate element at one end. Awanyu is the keeper of the springs, and in an arid area such as the Tewa Basin, preservation of the water supply is of paramount interest.

Though generally restricted approximately to the middle Rio Grande and Salinas provinces, by the mid-

Photo Archives, Museum of New Mexico.

dle 1500s red-slipped glaze-decorated pottery had made a sudden appearance in the Tewa Basin province at Puye Ruin, on the Pajarito Plateau west of Santa Clara Pueblo, and along the Rio Grande near modern San Juan Pueblo, just north of Española, New Mexico. Here it is too abundantly found to be accounted for only by trade. It would appear that some makers of glaze-decorated pottery—probably Tano, or southern Tewa people—must have moved into the Tewa Basin Province, bringing with them the glaze pottery technology.

Apparently their influence continued to be felt into the late 1600s, when the Tewa makers of Tsankawi Black-on-cream borrowed the idea of a red slip, applying it to the bottoms of their carbon-painted bowls and jars. The earliest known example of this merging of traditions is the bowl of Sakona Polychrome that was found in the side of a pipeline trench seven feet beneath the pavement of Lincoln Avenue on an old floor level of a long-demolished western part of the Palace of the Governors in downtown Santa Fe. With it was a single sherd of Fig Springs Polychrome, a majolica (i.e., tin-glazed earthenware) pottery imported from Mexico datable to the early 1600s. Thus, both the bowl and the floor level probably dated from a short time before the Pueblo Revolt of 1680, when the Pueblo Indians drove the Spanish colonists out of New Mexico for almost thirteen years.

Sakona Polychrome appears to be a long-standing Tewa tradition that persists to the present day. It may have had an effect on the pottery of the Keres- and Tiwa-speaking pueblos along the Rio Grande and its tributaries south of the Tewa Basin.

Following the reconquest of the Pueblos in the 1690s, the Spanish commandeered the lead mines that had provided the middle Rio Grande Anasazi with the pigments they needed for their glaze-decorated pottery. Deprived of this mineral, some of them switched to the widely available nonglazing iron pigments, while others chose to copy the carbon paint polychromes that the Tewa had developed.

With the advent of European household utensils during the Spanish, Mexican, and American periods, there probably were potters who practiced the craft less diligently. Metal, glass, and plastic replaced pottery in many Pueblo homes. By the early 1900s, there were fears that Pueblo pottery making would die out completely. However, some dedicated Pueblo potters continued to carry on the ancient traditions. Then, after World War II, the intrinsic value of Pueblo pottery became more widely recognized, encouraging a revitalization of the craft.

However, more recent developments in Pueblo pottery making have caused consternation among both Indians and non-Indians. They feel that commercially available clays, pigments, and kilns, the production of molded and purely decorative pots, and academic training in pottery making have no place in the pueblos and should not replace traditional ways. It is easy to see that the practice of pottery making in the prehistoric Southwest underwent numerous changes that may not have set well with all Anasazi and Mogollon. More changes are certain to come.

Historic and Contemporary Pueblo Pottery

RICK DILLINGHAM

Acoma Pueblo and Enchanted Mesa, New Mexico.
Photograph by Paul Logsdon.

BASKETRY AND CERAMIC CONTAINERS for the storage, preparation, and serving of food are part of the important material culture left behind by the ancestors of Pueblo Indians in New Mexico and Arizona. Basketry began with Archaic peoples around 5000 B.C., reaching an artistic and technical peak during the Pueblo III period (A.D. 900 to 1300). Pottery augmented basketry and by approximately A.D. 400 had gradually replaced it in the Anasazi Four Corners area for many culinary purposes. Time may have been a factor in this displacement of basketry: it takes far longer to weave a basket than to produce its pottery counterpart.

Early pottery forms were inspired primarily by natural containers such as gourds. The first designs painted on pottery were similar to those that had embellished baskets, but greater inventiveness in design motifs may be seen as the new craft began to be established. The design on a basket is not applied but woven into its substance, while pottery making offers the artist a prepared "canvas" upon which to explore a system of designs. As the potter became familiar with the possibilities of the material, forms and design systems unique to clay began to evolve, as they continue to evolve to this day. The ceramic medium offers virtually unlimited possibilities of producing forms to fit specific functions. The dictum that form follows function is particularly true of Pueblo pottery.

TYPE CLASSIFICATIONS

Pottery type classifications used by anthropologists, archaeologists, and collectors to determine date and place of manufacture are based on certain characteristics: the composition of the clay, the form of the vessel, the slips and paints, and the overall design. In studying large groups of pottery one can discern characteristics that constitute a norm. Site names and locations, given in Indian languages, are usually coupled with a distinguishing technical property, as, for example, Zia Polychrome (a pot of three or more colors from Zia Pueblo) and San Ildefonso Black-on-red

(a black-painted, red-slipped pot made at San Ildefonso Pueblo). Because of their inconsistency and creativity, however, the work of Pueblo potters tends to escape this close classification.

FORM AND FUNCTION

Pueblo potters met the needs of function with specific forms. The function of a dough bowl could change when needed for other purposes, for example the bathing of a child. Various water jars had to be of a particular size and form so as not to be too cumbersome and heavy when full. Canteens, usually bulbous forms with two handles and a short spout, were made to carry water to the fields and on journeys (fig. 90). A "spare-tire" bulge was molded into the jar at many pueblos, possibly to serve as a handle. The type of Hawikuh Polychrome at Acoma, Ashiwi Polychrome at Zuni, and Santa Clara Blackware are all examples of pottery with this molded bulge (figs. 44, 93). Larger jars stored grains and were used to prepare foods. Many large Historic Period jars have survived to the present, remaining where they first were set in a corner of a dwelling, too heavy to be easily moved.

Large dough-mixing bowls were made when wheat breads were introduced during the Spanish period (fig. 85). Bowls made for piki dough (paper-thin corn-based bread) are of an intermediate size. Smaller bowls are used for serving food. Jars for storing seeds were made with small openings, because they could easily be covered to prevent the entrance of vermin. Clay drinking vessels and pitchers have been made for centuries, only recently being replaced by glass, plastic, and metal.

Pottery forms do not need to be beautiful or decorated to fill their primary purpose. To be serviceable they need simply to be properly constructed and well fired. Attractive as they may be, designs are not necessary from a functional point of view. An exception may be the designs on ceremonial vessels, used in private religious events, that may be more important than the jar itself. Ceremonial vessels may be jars used in daily activity, annotated for the occasion by design additions; or specially produced vessels in specific shapes. Since all aspects of Pueblo life are connected to an overall religious purpose, all pottery comes from a ceremonial base whether it is for a specific ceremony, use in the house, or for sale.

PUEBLO OF ORIGIN: FORM AND DESIGN

As pottery making was established throughout the Southwest, regional styles began to develop that now help archaeologists identify points of origin. Materials are even more important than style in this determination, as many design motifs were shared. The clay itself is the major identifying factor, and with the tempering agent (the nonplastic addition of

sand, ground sherds, or rock), paint (guaco or the residue of boiled plants, or mineral, the combination of guaco and a natural iron-bearing rock), design, and firing atmosphere each vessel receives a distinctive identity. The materials, mainly the clay, at each location have certain properties that render them unique. The type of squat seed jar made at Hopi with local materials would be very difficult to construct with the clay from Santa Clara (fig. 135). The Hopi clay is dense and compact, where that of Santa Clara is softer and needs thickness for strength. Also, the clay from San Ildefonso, with properties similar to that of Santa Clara, would pose many problems in producing a jar as thin as those from Acoma, where a dense, strong clay is available.

Distinctive styles in form and design of pottery are noted among peoples settling along the Rio Grande; the western pueblos of Acoma, Laguna, and Zuni;

Acoma women with elaborately decorated pots, ca. 1917.
Photo Archives, Museum of New Mexico.

and the Hopi mesas. This evolution of unique styles now associated with certain pueblos is of great interest. Throughout the Historic Period, specific regional styles developed and among the pottery-producing pueblos today distinct individual features predominate.

Successful local forms in the past and present have been copied. The concave base used on water jars in the Rio Grande area to facilitate steadiness and easier carrying on the head travelled from the eastern to the western pueblos and became a normal feature there by about 1700. The severe-shouldered water jar form from Santa Clara became a commercial item at the turn of this century at San Ildefonso because of its graceful and impressive visual quality. The wedding vase, commonly associated with San Juan and Santa Clara, has become a saleable form as far away as Hopi and Acoma (fig. 183). More recently, the "storyteller" figures inspired by the work of Cochiti

potter Helen Cordero are produced at other pueblos as an artistic effort and tourist curio. They evolved from a figurative tradition beginning in the mid 1800s at Cochiti Pueblo.

The designs applied to pots at each pueblo are perhaps what initially catch the eye. Forms are sometimes similar among the pueblos, but designs can sometimes be used to identify the Pueblo where a pot was made. This method is not infallible, since many designs have been cross-traded or copied. For example, Zia and Acoma/Laguna share many cultural ties and among these pueblos designs were shared, too. In such cases, it is necessary to examine the materials of the vessel to determine the pueblo of origin. Designs have travelled from pueblo to pueblo in waves. The Zuni "rainbird" motif, a stylized bird consisting of a combination of a scroll and pendant elements described by H. P. Mera in 1937 in *The Rain Bird:*

Potters from Cochiti Pueblo, showing their wares at Indian Market
in Santa Fe, New Mexico, 1980s. Photograph by Carolyn Wright,
courtesy Southwestern Association on Indian Affairs.

A Study in Pueblo Design, was adopted by most of the pueblos as early as the first part of the 1800s and altered to suit individual tastes and styles. Hopi feather motifs travelled from the western to the eastern Rio Grande pueblos from as early as the mid 1600s and were interpreted differently by each pueblo. More recently, the Mimbres-inspired feather pattern, originally revived by Julian Martinez in the 1920s at San Ildefonso, has become a popular contemporary motif at many pueblos, including Jemez and Santa Clara (fig. 183).

The exchange of ideas about form and design among potters of various pueblos energizes their art, for while the Pueblo culture is homogeneous in many ways, its members have demonstrated a certain receptivity to the ideas of outsiders, when deemed beneficial. This quality has enabled the Pueblos to survive in a rapidly changing modern world and at the same time retain a cultural identity. With specific reference to pottery this flexibility translates to the making of a ware or specific vessel to meet the demand of the times, whether it be for a storage jar for corn, a ceremonial vessel for private use, or a tourist trinket.

Pottery from the Historic Period reveals outside influences in addition to those felt within the Pueblo world. Soup bowls, candlesticks, and chalices were introduced by the Spanish and absorbed into Pueblo pottery production after the mid 1600s. These probably were made for the Spanish, who utilized locally made products instead of importing them from Mexico and Spain. With the coming of Anglo settlers and, later, tourists in the mid to late 1800s, many new forms were introduced, including pitchers, cups and saucers, pottery baskets, and wares with fluted rims, but Pueblo potters did not depart from their traditional designs. Still, introduced designs are noted: pomegranate flowers, the parrot common at Acoma and Zia via imported fabric, and the Acoma "Thunderbird" from the double-headed Hapsburg eagle. The entwined floral motifs with many different flowers on the same vines probably came from imported chintz fabric of India.

Many scholars and collectors believe that the introduction of new forms and the response to the growing tourist market yielded inferior wares and was the beginning of a period of decline. In the mid to latter part of the 1900s efforts were made to recapture the quality of past works. Gifted potters were recognized and became the inspiration for a renewed interest in quality. Among those are Nampeyo at First Mesa at Hopi at the turn of this century (fig. 135); Maria and Julian Martinez at San Ildefonso in the late teens (figs. 94, 155); Serafina Tafoya at Santa Clara in the 1920s (fig. 93); and Lucy M. Lewis and Marie Z. Chino at Acoma in the 1950s. Collectors wanted to know who the artists were, and pots began to be signed, a practice that ran contrary to Pueblo culture. Currently there is a tendency to put too much emphasis on the name of the artist and not enough on the technical ability demonstrated in a particular pot.

TECHNIQUE: RAW CLAY TO FINISHED POT

Pueblo pottery is not complicated in its materials and construction. The basic elements of earth, water, and fire are used in that order. However, this simplicity can be deceiving. To produce serviceable wares with minimal technology, the potter must cooperate completely with the materials. Attempts to push beyond the limits of the materials will result in failure.

Clays, slips, and temper vary among the pottery-producing pueblos. Formerly, to limit the need for hauling, the search for materials began in proximity to each pueblo. With today's ease of transportation potters can go further afield, locating and experimenting with various nonlocal materials to create an individual statement. The work of Lela and Luther from Santa Clara exemplifies fine pottery produced from materials not all obtained at the home pueblo, including various colored slips from as far away as Colorado (fig. 169).

Clays vary in plasticity or workability and each type has unique characteristics. Most clays when initially mined are not sufficiently malleable. Usually the addition of a temper is necessary to render the

San Ildefonso potter Julian Martinez gathering clay, ca. 1941.
At right, potter Maria Martinez prepares clay for making pottery.
Photo Archives, Museum of New Mexico.

clay body or paste workable. Temper also is added to insure even drying and minimize warpage and thermal shock during firing. Through trial and error a potter will come up with a favorable clay mixture which is then generally preferred, with minor variations, by other local potters, giving that pueblo its distinctive blend. After the clay is chosen, potters will have individual preferences as to its consistency, one person preferring to work the clay very wet and another quite dry.

Recently, commercially prepared clays have offered a solution to impurities found in the locally mined material. This is in response to the collector's market, which often has steered the accommodating potter into new territory within the medium. Clays naturally have impurities and no matter how much a potter tries to screen and extract foreign material, inevitably there will be inclusions. Zia, San Ildefonso, and Acoma are three pueblos which have encountered intrusive gypsum material or limestone in their clay. This material, upon taking on atmospheric moisture after the firing, will pop from expansion, leaving small pits which may affect aesthetics but not serviceabili-

ty. Commercially prepared clay will not pit and is therefore now being used, especially at Acoma.

Among the Pueblos the most common method of building the vessel is by coiling and scraping. First, a base or support for construction is needed. The base portion of a previously made jar or a dish custom-made for a particular form (called a *puki*) is used. Potters today may employ commercially made dishes to serve this same purpose. The *puki* offers the clay support and the potter a turning base to facilitate construction of even vessel walls. (Until some recent student experiments Pueblo potters have never used the potter's wheel for traditional "old style" pottery.)

The walls of a vessel are made by the careful addition of ropelike coils of clay, successive coils being added either to the inside or the outside of the previous coil. This placement affects the overall profile of the vessel. The preceding coil must be sufficiently dry to sustain the weight of the next. A jar can easily cave in from the weight of coils not properly set.

Two of the most difficult forms to make are the shouldered jars typical of Santa Clara and San Ildefonso and the sharp shouldered seed jars from Hopi. The

Maria Martinez making coiled pot at San Ildefonso. From left:
working clay into coils; shaping the vessel by scraping pottery walls;
burnishing. Photographs by Tyler Dingee, ca. 1950.
Photo Archives, Museum of New Mexico.

tight welding of the coils is very important as each joint offers a potential place to crack. A homogeneous construction is essential to the survival of the final test of the fire. Once the jar is molded and at a "leather hard" stage, it is then scraped to its final shape and thinness with pieces of metal cans, wood, corncobs, and various other tools. Sandstone as well as commercial sandpaper have been used to smooth the overall surface when it is dry.

At the dry stage a pot can be fired and rendered serviceable. These vessels unslipped and unpainted are commonly called utility ware. At this stage, at many of the pueblos, a slip, clay watered down to a creamlike consistency used to change the color and/or texture of the surface of the vessel, may be applied. Slips can be indicative of the pueblo of origin but are known to have been traded in the past and are traded today. The slip used for many redwares made at Santa Clara is from Santo Domingo and the white slip used since about 1905 at San Ildefonso was obtained from Cochiti. The treatment of the surface and slip varies greatly from one pueblo to another. The highly polished wares associated with Santa Clara and

San Ildefonso are slipped with a fine red clay and rubbed with a worn stone to align the clay particles to reflect light. The addition of lard to the surface while polishing results in a mirror-like surface. In contrast, a softer, stone-polished finish is noted at Zia, Acoma, and Laguna. Rag-wiped slips, satiny in appearance, are used at Cochiti and Santo Domingo.

The process of painting designs also varies among the pueblos. Some use mineral paints, some slip paints, and other carbon (guaco) paints. These can also be used in combination. The mineral paints used by many potters are prepared on a stone palette. The natural hematite rock is mixed with the appropriate quantity of the vegetal material or guaco to produce a proper mixture. A mixture rich in mineral pigments may flake off after firing, while one containing too much vegetal material will be watery and thin. The paint is usually applied with the chewed end of a strip of yucca fiber. Today commercial paintbrushes are used by many potters for filling in areas of design. The quality of the yucca brush, however, is unmatched for the fine continuous line it offers on a curved vessel wall.

Some potters outline the design in black pigment and then fill areas with colored slips. These are usually set or fixed to the pot with a polishing stone, then outlined again where color has spilled over. Small pottery bowls are used to hold the colored slips, which can be reconstituted when dry. Guaco can be stored for years, becoming usable with the addition of water.

Designs, drawn in sections, are blocked out on the vessel, in the past with a piece of charcoal and in recent practice with pencil. The carbon of the initial outline burns off in the firing. Not all potters need to block out designs; many can draw freehand with confidence. At some pueblos, framing lines around the rim and the base are used as guidelines along the vertical panel lines. When the piece is dry it is ready to be fired. A piece has to be *absolutely* dry to survive the initial heating of the fire or else the potter will hear the disappointing sounds of steam mounting and popping out a portion of the vessel to make its escape. To insure absolute dryness potters place their wares around small fires to burn out the excess moisture before firing. Today many put them in the oven at a low temperature overnight.

Fuels for firing vary among the pueblos. Coal was used exclusively in the past at Hopi and still occasionally is sprinkled among the contemporary fuel of sheep manure. Sheep manure, "mined" in blocks from corrals and cut to manageable sizes, also is used at Laguna, Acoma, Zia, Hopi, and Zuni. Many potters purchase sheep manure by the truckload from Navajo shepherds. Corral-packed cow manure can be used in the same manner. Fluffy cow manure found on the open range is used by many potters, specifically at San Ildefonso and Santa Clara. Sawmill scraps of pine also are used by potters at Santa Clara. Split cedar logs are used at Cochiti, and at Santo Domingo the logs are used in combination with cow manure. Parts of the cottonwood tree and cedar splits have been used at Taos. The variations in fuels among the pueblos impart distinctive characteristics to the fired vessels. Corral-packed sheep manure generally burns hotter than cow manure from the open range. Both manure fuels leave an insulating ash residue to help with slow cooling. Pine and cedar create a fast, hot fire, and

coal, the hottest, is no longer used by pueblo potters with the exception at Hopi mentioned above.

The firing of pottery is a short process, taking only a few hours, but careful monitoring of the firing is exhausting and those hours are intense. The ware is stacked on grating, made from old pottery sherds or specially made pottery baffles, to allow for even air circulation and heating. Many potters use metal pieces such as license plates and old cafeteria trays. At least one contemporary potter at Hopi uses slabs of asbestos. The pottery is placed lip to foot, with the openings facing down to hold the heat generated by the fire. The ware is then covered with more pieces of metal or potsherds to form a fairly tight chamber. The chamber also serves as protection to prevent ash from falling on the pottery, producing fireclouds or smoky blemishes. Fuel is then placed around the structure and ignited. Many potters place a bed of kindling beneath the pottery and others simply ignite the fuel, often with the aid of a little charcoal lighter. This structure produces a sort of "self-consuming" kiln. The amount of time and quantity of fuel must be judged intuitively. The potter, through much experience, can tell by the color of the glowing pot when the piece is done.

Methods of firing vary at each pueblo. The length of the firing and degree of heat are very crucial when firing the black or red polished wares, trademarks of San Juan, San Ildefonso, and Santa Clara pueblos. A little too much heat will dull the lustrous polish. To obtain the black associated with Santa Clara and San Ildefonso, the fire is smothered at its peak with finely powdered horse manure. This produces an atmosphere that replaces oxygen in the pottery with carbon from the smoke of the smothered fire. A layer of ashes sometimes is used to cover the firing, preventing smoke from escaping. The result, when carefully carried out, is an even, lustrous black surface.

Fires burn in combinations of reducing and oxidizing atmospheres. The warm mottled effect of many Hopi pots is the result of a combination of the two atmospheres. Fireclouds or smoky blemishes occur when fuel rests on a pot, cutting off the supply of oxygen. At times this may have been done intentionally, especially with plainwares from San Juan, where patterns from fireclouds form warm natural designs.

Recently many potters have resorted to the use of kilns. Kiln firing is done at Hopi, Acoma, Laguna, Zuni, Cochiti, Jemez, Zia, Santa Clara and San Ildefonso (redware only), Santo Domingo, Isleta, and probably others on occasion. The distinctive mottling of Hopi pottery and fireclouds on Taos and Picurís wares are lost in a kiln. The blackwares are more easily fired in the outdoor fashion. The main impetus to using kilns was collectors' complaints about fireclouds marring the design, especially at Acoma. Now many collectors are asking for outdoor-fired wares because kiln firing is not traditional. This conflict of opinion has many potters baffled. Because of the current competitive marketplace, collectors have had some influence on the production of wares. This is an unfortunate but inevitable trend.

In the following sections, main characteristics of the pottery from different pueblos are discussed. There are many exceptions within the work of each pueblo and it is impossible to discuss them all. I have made an effort to mention the variations that are exceptions where possible. Pueblo pottery has changed greatly over the years. One constant, until very recently with the introduction of commercial products and methods, has been the mode of manufacture. The greatest change has been in the alteration of the vessel to meet the needs of the now popular art and tourist market. The tradition of using natively mined and prepared materials with an outdoor-style firing is still adhered to by many potters. In most cases, the same clays have been used and prepared in the same way at each pueblo for hundreds of years.

HOPI

The clay at Hopi, particularly at First Mesa, is mined in chunks and ground to a cornmeal consistency so that it will absorb water readily. In its unfired state it ranges in color from light gray to dark gray, yellow-gray to yellow. Its fired color is warm yellow to red-orange. Sand occurs naturally in the mined clay and rarely is the addition of extra temper necessary. As a rule, pottery is not slipped; rather, it is "floated" by moistening the surface and rubbing it with a worn stone.

However, there are examples of slipped pottery at Hopi in some of the rare Payupki Polychrome types (1680 to 1780) and the Polacca Polychrome types (c. 1780 to 1910) that were likely made or influenced by Rio Grande migrants to the Hopi area during the Pueblo Revolt and re-Conquest. Polacca, a First Mesa village, gives its name to the Hopi slipware produced from 1780 to 1900. The slipped surfaces of Polacca Polychrome pieces tend to have a network of fine crackles due to the divergent shrinkage rates between the clay body and the added slip.

Acoma man, ca. 1930. Photograph by Witter Bynner. Photo Archives, Museum of New Mexico.

Floated surfaces on wares tend to be dense and have a satiny sheen. Many factors can alter the final appearance of the surface; for example, the use of a sandy clay, a new polishing stone, and the amount of water applied while polishing.

Hopi designs are unique, with stylized birds and parts of birds being prominent elements. The designs usually are painted in black (made from a mixture of guaco, the boiled residue of the Rocky Mountain bee plant, and natural minerals such as iron and manganese) and red slip paint. White kaolinitic slip also is used in the design.

ZUNI

The clay at Zuni is mined in chunks from a sedimentary deposit. It is dark gray in its natural state and is ground to better absorb water. The temper used usually is ground potsherds; pottery hundreds of years old may be incorporated into a vessel. Sand has also been used for temper at Zuni. The slip is a white kaolinitic clay usually applied fairly thickly; however, if applied too thickly, it tends to form a discontinuous crackling. Until the mid 1800s a red slip was used on the bases of bowls and jars and on the interior rims of jars. This was supplanted by a brown-black slip that is still in use today.

The design catalog at Zuni is fairly limited, although there are endless variations of traditional designs. Designs are painted either overall or in banded patterns with the interruption of vertical panels and rosettes. In most cases the neck is designed separately. The black is a mixture of guaco and natural minerals and the red is a slip. Geometric elements with scrolls are common. The design most associated with Zuni is a semirealistic deer motif with a line leading from the heart to the mouth. This is most often called the "heart-line" deer.

ACOMA AND LAGUNA

A magnificent Acoma jar of Hawikuh Polychrome, dating from around 1680, marks the end of

Laguna potter during firing process, ca, 1915. Photographs by Harold Kellogg (left), Herman S. Hoyt. Photo Archives, Museum of New Mexico.

the glazeware period as well as the end of rounded bases (fig. 44). This type of pottery was also made at Zuni. The use of glazes in decoration began in the Zuni area approximately in the 1200s and somewhat later along the Rio Grande. This pottery was characterized by a vitreous lead-bearing glaze paint in colors ranging from green to purple and dark brown-black. Used principally for decorative purposes, it does not completely seal and waterproof the surface of a vessel. After about 1700, matte paints begin to be used at Acoma and Zuni.

The clay used at both Acoma and Laguna is roughly the same, with that at Laguna being a deeper shade of gray when mined. The clay is pulverized and ground potsherds are added as temper. Occasionally at Laguna volcanic rock and sand are added.

The slips used also are similar, a white kaolinitic clay applied and stone-polished. The white slip is sometimes applied more thickly at Laguna, with obvious stone marks, but it does not crackle as at Zuni. White slips can be applied quite thinly and still offer an even white background to receive the design. Various shades of yellow to red and occasional gray slips are used in the designs. The bases of jars and bowls are orange to orange-red, with the interior rims of the jars in the same slip as the base. Black rim tops replaced red ones and have been common at Acoma and possibly at Laguna since 1730 to 1740. Red-slipped bowl interiors appear to be more common at Laguna than at Acoma, where undecorated white slip is typical.

Acoma and Laguna designs are among the most elaborate of the Pueblo potters. Many are shared, and determining the pueblo of origin can be difficult. Painted in mineral black and colored slips, they fall into two basic types: banded and allover (fig. 77). The banded designs follow the zones of construction, with a neck band and possibly shoulder and body bands, which may be further divided. The allover patterning employs a design running continuously from the lip to the foot.

The parrot is a familiar design element in Acoma ceramics and may have been suggested by imported trade cloth (fig. 52). The bird and floral motifs appear too well developed to have been arrived at through a slow evolution. Potters also have exactly reproduced elements from New Mexican colcha embroidery of the Colonial Period.

The geometric motifs, especially from 1880 to the present, tend to cover entirely the surface of the pot, dividing and redividing the designs. Prehistoric designs from other cultures, mainly the Hohokam and the Mimbres, have been used in recent times as a commercial effort.

COCHITI AND SANTO DOMINGO

As with Acoma and Laguna, the differences between wares of these two pueblos are difficult to discern. The clays are of a sandy consistency when mined and the temper is a volcanic tuff. Occasionally the clay contains soft white gypsumlike inclusions and some crystalline rock. The slip is a bentonitic clay with very fine particles that stick to the stone if stone polished. It is applied with a rag or a piece of leather and later rubbed with a rag or the palm of the hand. If applied too thickly it tends to peel up,

much as the clay in a dry lake bed. Red slips have also been used. Bases are floated and until around 1930 they had an underbody band of red-orange slip. This band possibly was an abbreviation of the earlier allover red-slipped bases of pottery, but this is speculation. At Cochiti and Santo Domingo the band is applied thinly and is polished. It tends to be wider, a deeper orange, and less well polished than the corresponding feature of Tewa pottery to the north. Red rim tops gave way to black in the early 1800s. From the 1920s to the 1940s potters at Santo Domingo experimented with the Black-on-black style which was receiving much attention at San Ildefonso.

At these Pueblos designs are executed with a carbon black paint or the boiled residue of the bee plant (guaco). This paint on the bentonitic slip can range from deep black to watery grey. The designs at Santo Domingo tend more toward the geometric, with bird and floral elements as well (fig. 85). Red is rarely used in the design. Cochiti designs are fussier, with many free-floating elements and sketchy details, and ceremonial motifs such as clouds and lightning. Red is used more frequently in the Cochiti designs, many of which have an almost whimsical effect.

ZIA AND SANTA ANA

The clay used at Zia and Santa Ana is a sandy-textured reddish-brown clay that fires to a red-orange color. The temper used at both pueblos is a water-worn sand; the addition of a ground basalt (black fleck) is distinctive at Zia. The white slips (sometimes buff at Zia) have a chalky quality, as does the red slip used in the design. Occasionally a mustard-yellow slip is used in the design at Zia. The bases of bowls and jars are floated with the addition of the underbody band. Bases of some Zia pots are entirely slipped in red and polished. The underbody band is sometimes painted in the same slip and left unpolished, creating only a slight difference in texture. Red slips are painted on the interior of jar rims, and red rims were common into the late 1700s.

Zia pottery designs are very distinctive in the

use of bird motifs and the undulating "rainbow" band, encircling many jars with bird and floral motifs (figs. 51, 141). These designs probably have connections to Colonial Colcha embroidery. Geometric designs also are common. There are great similarities between Zia designs and those of Acoma and Laguna. Deer elements painted in a fairly realistic style are also Zia trademarks (fig. 87). Designs at Santa Ana are perhaps the most distinctive of all the pueblos, with bold thick painting in red and black (fig. 78). They have an architectural scale and do not seem to have been influenced by non-Indian elements or other pueblos.

SAN ILDEFONSO AND TESUQUE

Clay used at these pueblos is very similar to that used at Santo Domingo and Cochiti. The temper added is also a volcanic tuff, commonly called "sand." Regional tempering variations occur but are so light as to be difficult to distinguish. The treatment of the white slip is a feature distinguishing this ware from that of Cochiti and Santo Domingo. It is stone-stroked rather than rag-wiped and stone marks are noticeable on the surface along with occasional fine crackling. It appears that at Tesuque more than at San Ildefonso the surface of the pottery becomes rippled by the action of stone-stroking. This result also may reflect the potter's skill.

The bases of jars and bowls are smoothly floated with dense, thin red underbody bands. Both pueblos have used red slips on the bodies of the vessels as well. The red slip at San Ildefonso and perhaps Tesuque is a combination of the white body slip and a dense red slip yielding a soft red. Around 1905 Cochiti slip was introduced at San Ildefonso by Martina and Florentino Montoya to speed up the slipping process and eliminate the laborious stone-stroking, in order to meet new tourist demands. It was used until the Black-on-black technique commanded the attention of the public. Maria and Julian Martinez used the Cochiti slip in their polychrome work and some other potters have experimented with it recently. The rim tops on the bowls and jars were red until about 1900 to 1915 with some pieces in the Cochiti slip being

painted black. The Black-on-black technique involves an initial overall polishing of the vessel with red slip. Then, using a thinned mixture of slip, designs are painted over the polished surface. Before the firing the jar is a matte red-brown on polished red; and after the firing the more recognizable matte and polished black.

Designs at San Ildefonso are a combination of geometric and fluid curvilinear elements (fig.101). Red is used often in the designs that regularly are painted in a banded configuration. Bird and floral motifs also are used. The black paint is carbon, as it is at Tesuque. With the "invention" of the Black-on-black style designs tended to become more geometric and carefully drawn. Julian Martinez was instrumental in bringing Hopi, Mimbres, and other designs to the vocabulary. The design that became his trademark, and that of San Ildefonso Pueblo as well, is the Avanyu or water serpent, a common motif associated with water and fertility. Tesuque's designs are more similar to those of Cochiti with which they are often confused. They tend to be fussy and have an overall "spikey" feel to them (fig. 80). They usually are painted in a banded pattern and rarely use red in the design.

SANTA CLARA AND SAN JUAN

It was very difficult to distinguish the pottery from these two pueblos until the demand from the tourist market stimulated distinctions. The clay at both pueblos is similar to that from San Ildefonso and Tesuque. Santa Clara did not develop a polychrome tradition, except for experiments by Serafina Tafoya and her son Manuel in the 1920s and the work of Lela and Van Gutierrez in the 1930s and '40s. Other potters have experimented with polychromes at Santa Clara in recent times as a commercial venture. The pueblo preserved a plainware tradition that has been in existence since the 1700s (fig. 93). The pottery is slipped in red and fired in an oxygen-reducing atmosphere to penetrate the vessel with carbon, resulting in a blackware. Rare redwares also were made by not smothering the fire.

Potters at San Juan Pueblo, ca. 1935. Photograph by T. Harmon Parkhurst. Photo Archives, Museum of New Mexico.

Potters at San Juan followed the same basic procedure as the potters at Santa Clara. One distinction between the two is that potters at San Juan often slipped only the upper one-half to two-thirds of water and storage jars, creating a two-tone effect either in redware (orange and red) or blackware (gray-brown and black). This style in blackware is also noted at Santa Clara and perhaps Nambé, where little pottery is done today. The bowl shape associated with San Juan—a round bottom and concave sides—is a carry-over from the 1700s and was made into the early 1900s. Modelled figures of animals, wedding vases, and candlesticks were popular tourist items when the railroad reached the southwest and are still made. Innovations, now traditions, from the 1920s and 1930s at both pueblos include the deep carved wares of Santa Clara and the incised design work with inlaid mica slip and bas relief carving at San Juan. Potters at Santa Clara also made the Black-on-black style popular at San Ildefonso. (fig. 140). Sgraffito carving, or the shallow "scratched" removal of slip from the clay body, has become a very popular design technique. It originated at San Ildefonso with potter Popovi Da, but recently has become more a trademark of Santa Clara. The technique has become very elaborate, with multicolored slips, colored pigments, and set stones. Technical prowess in polishing and firing have become the hallmark of pottery making at Santa Clara.

TAOS AND PICURÍS

The wares of Taos and neighboring Picurís and of the Apaches are made from a clay naturally tempered with inclusive mica. This clay needs no extra temper and is a highly durable ware suited for cooking. Taos pottery is decorated not by painting but rather with added coils in simple geometric or more fluid patterns (fig. 144). Serviceable utility ware continues to be produced today and is perhaps the only ware still being made for uses other than ceremonial. The firing of the pottery adds its own design where the fuel touches the ware, leaving a fire cloud or grey-black area.

Though each pueblo has distinctive pottery, all are part of a larger culture based on living traditions. Tradition is a growing, living process that both preserves and evolves the information, beliefs, and customs of the past. It is an indivisible part of the fabric of life and can no more be separated from it than can a ceramic vessel be beheld apart from its design. Tradition does not refer necessarily to that which is old or antique; traditions are started every day, with pottery making as with any cultural activity. Traditional modes of manufacturing pottery once meant the mining and preparation of native materials and the firing of wares with local fuels. Because the function of the pottery has changed and is now made for sale to the tourist and art collector, the modes of manufacture also have changed. The carved black pottery of Santa Clara, now a traditional ware, was introduced around 1924–26 by Serafina Tafoya. At the time it was first made it must have seemed quite innovative, but now it is mainstream traditional Santa Clara pottery. What is original and different now may in time be regarded as traditional, as the Pueblo potter continues to revitalize an ancient art.

Southwestern Indian Jewelry

NANCY FOX

Chetro Ketl ruin at Chaco Canyon, New Mexico.
Photograph by Paul Logsdon.

THE DESIRE FOR PERSONAL ADORNMENT seems to be a universal human attribute. It is therefore reasonable to suppose that it existed among the Southwest's earliest inhabitants, who have left us a few examples of their stone tools but little else to illuminate their artistic tastes. Nor have there been discovered surviving examples of the ornaments which may have been fashioned by the big game hunters who followed now-extinct animal species across the plains of New Mexico, Colorado, and Arizona at the end of the last great Ice Age. They left behind evidence of their unsurpassed skill in the art of stone chipping—Folsom, Clovis, and other types of superbly crafted spear points which provide ample proof of their artistic abilities. But no stone or bone jewelry has been found in an identifiable Early Man context. We can only surmise that their adornments, if they existed, may have been fashioned from some less durable materials.

The hunter-gatherers from farther south, bearers of the Desert tradition that contributed to the succeeding Mogollon, Anasazi, and Hohokam cultures in the first millennium B.C., made jewelry that has endured the passage of time: simple but handsome beads and pendants of stone, bone, horn, shell, tooth, claw, and even vegetal materials like bark and yucca

Mask adorned with eagle feathers, resembling Pueblo sun deity Ahul, from a Navajo petroglyph found in the Navajo Reservoir District. From *Rock Art in New Mexico*, by Polly Schaafsma.

fiber. Many were prototypes of jewelry that later was refined and elaborated and that still exists in the Southwest of the present day.

Following is a brief survey of pre-Spanish Indian jewelry as discovered among the major southwestern cultures—Anasazi (Basketmakers and Pueblos), Hohokam, and Mogollon—as well as among groups dwelling in the greater Southwest. Especially influential among the latter were the prehistoric peoples of Casas Grandes, a vast ruin in Chihuahua, Mexico, and once a trading center through which many Mexican traits travelled northward into what is now the United States.

Every part of the body that lends itself to adornment, among them some not often decorated today, received the attentions of the prehistoric craftsman. Neck ornaments, then as now, were perhaps most universal, and they were fashioned in many forms from all available materials. Necklaces sometimes were very simple, composed of one strand of a single substance, such as stone disc beads or olivella shells. But they also might be intricate ornaments employing a variety of materials and manufacturing techniques and as many as one thousand beads or more.

Beads, pendant beads, and pendants, worn alone or to set off the bottom of a necklace, were common to every culture and every period, though styles and materials varied. Beads could be disc-shaped, barrel-like, globular or tubular, cylindrical, irregular, or unshaped. One interesting variation consisted of a bilobed or figure eight–shaped outline which, when worn, created the effect of a double strand. Beads were drilled and strung either centrally or longitudinally or, as in the case of tubular beads made by sectioning animal long bones, strung through the natural cavity. Occasionally, if the cavity did not provide the desired closeness of fit, a smaller bead might be wedged inside.

Pendants included flat geometric forms, odd forms such as the sliver of a bivalve shell rim, and life forms or effigies, both human and animal, especially fine examples of which are the mountain sheep pendant from near Casas Grandes, Chihuahua (fig. 36), and a Hohokam shell frog effigy (fig. 15). Pen-

Edgar Lee Hewett, archaeologist and founder of the Museum of
New Mexico, at Casas Grandes, Chihuahua, Mexico, 1922.
Photograph by Kenneth Chapman. Photo Archives,
Museum of New Mexico.

dants were perforated with one or more holes at one end, or at each end if a horizontal ornament was intended. Sometimes the pendant was notched, or grooved all around, and the suspension cord tied into place. A very large form of pendant, worn over the chest, was called a gorget. Usually these were made of stone or shell. Abalone shell, due both to its size and its considerable beauty, was particularly well suited to use in this type of ornament.

A variety of arm ornaments apparently vied with necklaces in popularity. Bracelets (also rings) were carved from shell, stone, and bone, the most common type of bracelet being formed from a large glycymeris shell with a cut-out center. They also were fashioned of perishable materials such as wood or twigs. Short strings of beads were used to adorn arms or wrists, sometimes with attached charms or amulets.

One form of arm ornament, the bow or wrist guard, served a double purpose. It was not only decorative, but it protected the wearer's wrist from the snap of the bowstring, and therefore usually was worn on the wrist to be shielded. However, it appears that there often was a favored side for the wearing of bracelets. For instance, shell bracelets were usually worn on the left forearm by the Mogollon inhabitants of Cameron Creek Village (Bradfield 1931). At Hawikuh, an Anasazi site predating Zuni Pueblo (Hodge 1921), bow guards were worn on the right wrist and bracelets of turquoise were worn on the left.

As with bracelets, traditions also existed in regard to earrings. At Hawikuh, males wore loops of minute turquoise beads, usually only in the left ear. Women, on the other hand, wore ear tablets decorated with turquoise mosaics. Similar tablets continued to be worn by Zuni and Hopi maidens into historic times. Ear ornaments varied in form and in degree of decoration. Besides tablets and loops, geometric and effigy pendants have been found, as well as rings, buttons, and plugs.

Lip ornaments (labrets) and nose buttons and plugs of wood and stone were in fashion among the Hohokam and also were found at hybrid sites such as Ridge Ruin (McGregor 1943) and Kinishba (Mott 1936).

Hair and head ornaments were fabricated in a great variety of pins, combs, and bands, in addition to various shaped headdresses, many of ceremonial nature. Some of these were further embellished with inlay or overlay. Wood and vegetal materials have been found, usually in fragmentary condition, which seem to have constituted headdresses of the sort seen in *tablitas* (headdresses) of the modern Pueblos. Frequently, such objects were further decorated by painting and with the attachment of feathers, pendants, or other ornaments, including antlers and horns, real and false. An exceptional example of beadwork discovered at Ridge Ruin is a sort of cap composed of concentric rows of minute beads: white shells strung alternately with gray and black stones. Southwest Indians hung clusters of feathers from their hair as well as from their garments. Tablets, pendants, and pins were attached to clothing, as were articles that have been identified variously as buttons, buckles, or brooches.

Modern Apache women trim the buckskin fringes of their skirts with tin "tinklers," which, when they move, produce a soft jingling sound. So, too, modern Pueblos, when dressing for ceremonial dances, attach bells or bits of shell to their waist, arms, or legs. Similar items, producing the same effect, were manufactured in the prehistoric Southwest. Tinklers made of shell and bells of clay or copper were worn as pendants or in necklaces and probably also were attached to garments. Tinklers in short strands were fastened around arms or legs, while long strands may have been sewn to leggings or perhaps tied along the length of the leg itself. Especially large glycymeris shells were suitable for use as leg ornaments or anklets

and were fashioned in the same way as bracelets. Sometimes, too, strands of beads were worn about the ankle.

Ornaments, then, were displayed from head to foot, adorning body and clothing alike, reflecting in both form and material variety the wide range of techniques evolved by the prehistoric craftsman. Substances used in the manufacture of jewelry were as diverse as local resources and conditions of trade allowed. Readily available in most areas, stone had from earliest times provided a reliable source of supply for the production of tools and implements of all kinds. Although shell was more easily worked and therefore was sometimes preferred for jewelry making, stone was used by every southwestern culture for this purpose, and among some groups it predominated over every other material.

Undoubtedly the one mineral prized above all was turquoise. Its use has been recorded since the earliest phases of Hohokam Culture, when its use seems to have spread rapidly northward and eastward. In southwestern Indian religions it has important associations, usually with sky and water, and the color often symbolizes one of the six directions (north, south, east, west, zenith, and nadir) recognized by a number of Indian groups.

Almost as important to many prehistoric Southwesterners were jet and lignite, both related to coal. Zunis call lignite "black turquoise." Light in weight and capable of attaining a high polish, it was utilized to make many types of ornaments: gorgets, pendants, or buttons. Lignite also was cut into tiny pieces for use in mosaic.

Mica was another mineral displayed in mosaic by the Hohokam. In the Rio Grande area, mica and selenite had many uses. It was fashioned into pendants and enjoyed popularity as distinctive dress ornaments, a use that remained popular into the 1600s (fig. 35).

Beads and pendants constituted the largest single class of stone ornament. Their manufacture involved a number of techniques, depending upon the final form desired. One of the most widespread forms was the disc. Larger in diameter than height,

TURQUOISE MINES OF THE SOUTHWEST

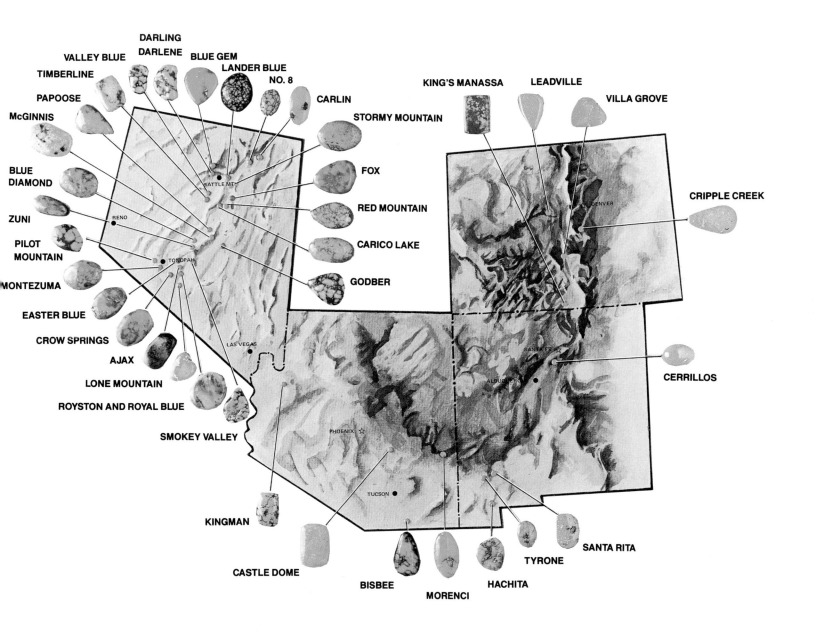

Approximate locations of the principal turquoise mines in Nevada,
Arizona, New Mexico, and Colorado. These stones were selected
from thousands to illustrate the most characteristic type and color of
a fine quality stone from each mine. Map by Oscar T. Branson from
Turquoise: The Gem of the Centuries, published by Treasure
Chest Publications, Tucson.

such beads were centrally perforated and strung side by side. An exceptionally fine assortment of black and white stone disc beads was recovered at Chetro Ketl, an Anasazi site in Chaco Canyon (fig. 1). Ten necklaces, wound into garlands, were discovered in ten sealed crypts within the wall of the Great Kiva, along with turquoise pendants, buttons, and thousands of tiny turquoise fragments—some seventeen thousand pieces in all. They were excavated in 1931 under the direction of the Museum of New Mexico director at that time, Edgar Lee Hewett, who stated that it was "probably the most precious, undisturbed ritualistic deposit ever found in American excavation" (Hewett 1936).

To make disc beads, a thin slab was formed by flaking along one edge; this was then ground to a uniform thickness. Small sections were then marked off by grooving on both faces, these were broken out, and the unfinished bead was perforated. Finally, the edges were shaped and smoothed by grinding. This last process could be applied to each individual bead if it was fairly large. But, especially in the case of tiny specimens, it was preferable to string the beads first. The whole strand could then be rubbed over an abrading stone, resulting either in a necklace that was precisely graduated, or in one that was uniform in shape and size.

Perforations in beads were of three general types. The most common was uniform in diameter throughout, the uniformity apparently achieved by means of a long slender implement upon which the bead could be rotated after drilling. A conical hole, on the other hand, indicates the use of a tapered drill. Many beads were drilled from both sides, the holes meeting to result in a biconical perforation. The drill used by the pre-Spanish craftsmen was probably a simple implement operated by revolving it in alternating directions between the hands. Modern Pueblo beadmakers use the pump drill, but according to Stubbs and Stallings in their monograph on Pindi Pueblo, it is doubtful that this implement was known in prehistoric America (see photo). Stone drills were by far the most common, although bead drills sometimes were made of cane or reed.

A special form of disc bead was the minute variety, ranging in size from tiny to nearly microscopic. These were made only in the Southwest and surpass in craftsmanship even the finest modern examples. While the basic steps of manufacture would be similar to those just described, the perforation of the minutest beads undoubtedly presented special problems. It is unlikely that stone, cane, or even bone could be worked into a drill sufficiently fine. Haury (1931) has suggested that the precision tool used for this purpose might have been derived from the spine of a local cactus, probably the barrel cactus or the saguaro. In his 1950 book on Ventana Cave, a site that demonstrated the great variety of uses to which vegetal materials could be put, Haury mentions the find of a cactus needle.

Minute beads were worn by the Hohokam, Anasazi, and Mogollon alike. They have been found in sites south from the San Juan River almost to the Mexican border. It is interesting to speculate on the length of time required to produce, for example, a necklace like the one found near Kayenta, Arizona, consisting of minute beads which, when strung, formed a necklace thirty-two feet long and averaging forty beads to the inch. Allowing fifteen minutes per bead (including collection and preparation of materials, making the drills, drilling, and final polish), Haury estimated that it would take a single individual approximately four hundred eighty eight-hour days to finish work on the fifteen thousand or more beads represented in that single necklace (Haury 1931). A mixture of dark gray and black beads with red ones (often made of hematite) seems to have been popular, for it is a combination which appears frequently in necklaces and ear loops of this type. Other widely utilized materials included turquoise and white shell.

Stone pendants were sometimes reinforced by more durable substances such as bone, if manufactured from some fragile stuff or in very thin sections. Choice of material was presumably influenced by availability, while cultural traditions dictated appropriate shapes. Occasionally concretions, occurring in odd natural forms, were suspended from the neck. The stages of pendant manufacture followed those of bead

San Felipe Pueblo man demonstrates the use of a pump drill to perforate beads, ca. 1880. Photo Archives, Museum of New Mexico.

which were more easily worked and therefore much more common. Such natural formations as concretions were sometimes fashioned into rings. Another type of stone bracelet or ring was formed from short strands of beads.

Stone earrings encompassed a variety of forms: pendants in geometric and effigy shapes, bead loops, tablets, and plugs or rings. Nose plugs and/or labrets were most frequently made of stone. In addition, stone was employed in the fabrication of buttons, buckles, and ornaments for hair and clothing.

Stone ornaments sometimes were adapted from articles originally manufactured for other purposes. Commonest among items of this type were projectile points, some representing much earlier cultures, picked up later and reused as amulets or pendants.

Aside from the decorative quality inherent in the form, color, and texture of stone ornaments, additional decoration was applied by means of designs that were incised, cut out, or carved in relief and then painted. Carved and incised stone was found among all cultures, but the greatest variety was achieved by the Hohokam.

Among the most beautiful southwestern ornaments were those enhanced by the application of incrustation and inlay. Several variations existed. In some cases, one or more pieces of stone (or shell), geometric or zoomorphic in outline, were overlaid on a larger, shaped background. An elaboration of this technique involved the construction of intricate mosaics in which each tiny piece was cut to fit exactly and the edges often bevelled for greater precision. Inlay, in contrast to overlay, involved carving out the design in the backing, then inserting pieces of stone and other substances cut precisely to shape. Several materials might form the base for inlay and incrustation. Stone, shell, wood, bone, and, less frequently, ceramic ornaments were decorated in this way. Often, too, less durable materials such as basketry, wood, reed, or other vegetal materials served as backings. The techniques of overlay and inlay are as popular today as in the prehistoric past. A modern example of incrustation, for instance, may be seen in the tobacco horns pictured in figure 156.

making: a suitable piece of stone was ground thin by abrasion, shaped as desired, then drilled near one or more extremities. A pendant found at Pueblo Bonito, another magnificent ruin in Chaco Canyon (Pepper 1920), demonstrates the skill of the craftsman in matters of technology. It had been carved in the form of an animal effigy from a soft pink and white stone and inlaid with turquoise. To prevent the suspension cord from cutting into the soft stone, as it would have done if perforated in the ordinary manner, a bird bone was inserted in a hole drilled just above the neck. The opening on each side was countersunk and the space filled with gum. A large turquoise bead had then been fastened over each end, completely covering the bone.

Bracelets and rings sometimes were carved from stone. These usually imitated those made of shell,

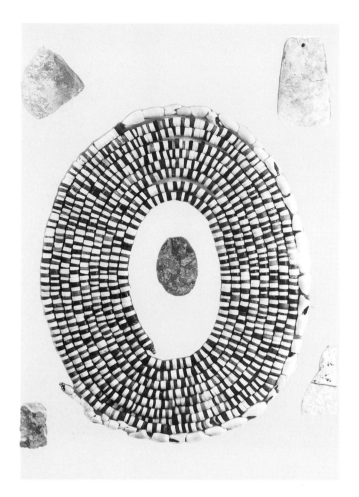 

Anasazi necklaces, ca. 1050, found in the Great Kiva at Chetro
Ketl, Chaco Canyon, New Mexico. The one on
the left contains 1,538 beads and measures 10½ feet. The other
contains 1,940 beads and is 11¾ feet long.

Mosaic apparently was one of the decorative techniques which reached the Southwest from Mexico and Central America. Its appearance among the Hohokam seems to predate its arrival among the Anasazi. However, it had been incorporated into that culture at least by late Basketmaker times.

Adhesives varied from group to group, partly due to factors such as availability. Gummy substances like piñon pitch were widely favored. One of the most interesting was lac, exuded by the lac insect, which inhabits certain plants native to the desert Southwest. It is the basis of such modern products as shellac, sealing wax, and dye. Excavations at Ridge Ruin provided the first known instance of its use in prehistoric America.

Both because of its natural beauty and because it was easier to work than stone, shell was employed extensively in the manufacture of jewelry. In the Southwest, it was used almost solely for this purpose. Both marine and freshwater shells were utilized, although marine varieties predominated by far. The presence of marine shells in the Southwest indicates a widespread trade, the chief source being the Gulf of California.

Shells selected for ornament included bivalves (clams, mussels, oysters, scallops, cockles) and also gastropods of many kinds. Colorful species like the spiny oyster were well suited to the production of jew-

These fine examples of prehistoric jewelry from the Great Kiva
contain 1,724 and 1,797 beads respectively and measure 12½ feet
and 14 feet. The one on the right contains turquoise.

elry. Above all, the iridescent abalone provided a rare and highly prized material for pendants, gorgets, and mosaics. Also utilized were fossilized marine remains such as crinoid stems and fossil coral.

Vast quantities of shell beads and pendants have been recovered from southwestern sites. These were among the easiest kinds of ornament to manufacture, as a shell could simply be pierced and strung in its natural state. Beads made of olivella shells, with their spires ground off for stringing through the canal, were among the most common of all southwestern types. Shells like conus and olivella were sometimes truncated at each end or ground into barrel, saucer, rectangular, tubular, or disc shapes (figs. 1, 36).

The process of manufacture was similar to that used for stone beads. The shell was cut into slabs and the slab notched with a series of incised lines in checkerboard fashion; these broke easily into rough squares, which were then drilled and strung. If a disc was intended, the bead was rubbed back and forth in a grooved stone until the desired shape was achieved. To produce a square, it was drawn across a flat slab of an abrasive material such as sandstone in order to straighten and smooth the sides (Ezell 1937). Pendants and beads were carved into various geometric shapes, effigies, and the figure-eight form previously noted. Designs were incised and carved on both pendants and beads, the carving probably executed

Mimbres necklace from the Osborn Ruin, 1000–1150, is
composed of alternating sections of red and black stone, each section
divided by a white shell bead. Mogollon Necklace, 850–900. Heavy
discoidal beads made from mottled pinkish-white bivalve shells,
from the Tunis site, New Mexico. Photographs by Blair Clark.

with a flint chip. Drills, too, usually were made of chipped stone. Because shell did not break as easily as did stone during drilling, a larger drill could be used; for this reason, the perforations in shell beads generally were larger than those in stone.

Minute beads were fashioned from shell as well as from stone. The use of shell both in the composition of and as a base for mosaic has been noted earlier. Bivalves decorated with mosaic made splendid pendants and gorgets. Painted shell, while not common, had a multicultural distribution and was found in articles such as pendants, effigies, bracelets, and armlets.

Glycymeris shells frequently had their centers ground away, the remaining circular rim forming an anklet, a bracelet, or a ring, depending upon the size of the shell. Usually the outer rims were left unworked to preserve the natural fluting. While many were plain, others had decorated rims or displayed carved umbos, often in effigy form. Sometimes the umbos were pierced for the attachment of another ornament. The two bracelets illustrated in figure 16, from Cameron Creek Village, are elaborately carved; such near matching pairs were rare indeed. Rings were some-times formed from a section of a conus shell. Inlay, though more commonly in pendants and ear bobs, also was used to decorate bracelets and rings. Occasionally it might be combined with carving.

In addition to its use in bracelets, shell was combined with other materials to form composite wrist ornaments such as shell-decorated bow guards. Earrings usually took the form of cut shell pendants. Another type, found among the Hohokam, was a ring-shaped shell ear plug which resembled the kind made of stone. Tinklers were made by grinding away the whorl end of the conus shell, creating a flat-bottomed cone. The small end was then perforated for suspension. Occasionally olive shells were used for this type of ornament, but evidently conus was preferred.

Decoration on shell was produced by carving, painting, inlay, or overlay in the form of mosaic. However, one of the most interesting as well as sophisticated techniques—and one of the rarest—was a method of etching shell, apparently invented by the Hohokam. It was used only by them and only for a relatively short period of time. The method may be reconstructed as follows: the shell was first covered with gum or pitch, leaving certain parts exposed; it was then placed in a weak solution of acetic acid, possibly fermented from the fruit of the saguaro cactus, which ate away the exposed portion to produce the desired effect.

The introduction of pottery was one of the traits heralding development of the great cultures of the prehistoric Southwest. It is not surprising, therefore, that ceramics should have been adapted for personal adornment. Pottery vessels are breakable, as the quantities of potsherds found at archaeological sites amply testify. But broken fragments were not always discarded. They could be reused in a variety of ways: Some became scrapers, polishers, or spindle whorls, and some were worked into pendants, in many shapes. Sometimes they display only a plain surface, sometimes a bit of design. Lugs and portions of effigy vessels were at times selected for reuse as pendants.

Ceramic jewelry, however, was by no means limited to reworked pottery. Clay ornaments were manufactured in some abundance, especially by the Anasazi. Clay beads, although not as common as those fashioned from shell and stone, occurred in globular, cylindrical, and disc forms, as well as in several more unusual shapes.

Ordinarily, such beads were made in one of two ways. Each bead might be molded individually around a piece of vegetal fiber. Or a grass stem or other suitable piece of vegetal fiber was encased in a thin layer of wet clay, forming a tube which was then sectioned at intervals by shallow incisions. This was allowed to dry and was then fired, consolidating the clay and destroying the fiber. Finally, the individual beads were broken loose at the incisions and their edges were either rubbed or left unsmoothed (Haury 1931).

A unique pendant in the collections of the Laboratory of Anthropology, found at the Rio Grande site of Los Aguajes, consists of a clay replica of a cockle shell. Its polished, reddish-tan slip is painted with longitudinal red lines in imitation of ribbing.

Beads and pendants together account for most ceramic jewelry. But other forms of clay ornament were produced in lesser amounts, including nose plugs, possible lip plugs, and dress ornaments.

Although less widely distributed than bells made of copper, clay bells doubtless were worn in the same ways as the metal ones. Pecos Pueblo (Kidder 1932) provided examples of two types, both apparently late. They were made of brown paste, unslipped and unpainted. Most were globular and thick-walled, so that the clay pellet inside produced a dry rattling sound. To form this variety, the clay was molded into a ball and provided with a lipped opening through which an implement could be inserted to hollow it. The clapper was placed inside and the lips then pushed together, while the top was punched to provide a flat surface which could be drilled for suspension. Some bells, though, were larger and "flat," having been molded entirely by hand and folded over the pellet. Their lighter walls produced a sharper sound. They too were drilled for suspension.

Metal ornaments generally were unknown during pre-Spanish periods. The one notable exception was copper, used almost exclusively for the production of cast copper bells, objects which most likely entered the Southwest from Mexico. Early bells throughout the Southwest were usually globular or pear-shaped. Pueblo IV bells were larger and some of them incorporated such innovations as appliqué. Tiny stone pebbles or copper pellets were used as clappers. Copper bells appear to have served much the same purpose as shell tinklers. They were suspended as pendants or attached to clothing. The relatively scarce material also was used by pre-Spanish craftsmen for making beads. A necklace with three beaten copper beads was discovered at Aztec Ruin in northern New Mexico (Morris 1919). Other ornaments, such as a pair of effigy pendants from the Mimbres Valley, carved from flat sheets of copper, are preserved in the School of American Research Collections in the Museum of New Mexico.

Plentiful in most areas, easily worked, and capable of use in a variety of ways, wood and other vegetal materials have been employed extensively for purposes of ornamentation throughout all periods of history. It is regrettable that due to their perishable nature, examples tend to be poorly preserved in most southwestern archaeological sites. Without doubt, this type of jewelry was much more common than extant specimens would indicate.

Vegetal fiber cordage and basketry were fashioned into ornaments, as were gourds, seeds, nuts, reed or cane, and wood. Among agricultural peoples it is not surprising to find ornamental utilization of domesticated plants such as corn. The Basketmakers, for instance, sometimes used corn husk to make a decorative outer wrapping for cordage in necklaces. The Mogollon occasionally folded corn husk itself into ornaments. Simple rings were easily formed of grass or twigs, and also from the seed pods of a plant called Devil's Claw.

Walnut shells and acorn cup beads were strung as necklaces, as were seeds of many types. Seeds were sometimes combined with other materials, as in seed-and-shell-decorated wrist ornaments found at Hawikuh. Seed necklaces were popular throughout the Southwest at various times, and were especially plentiful at Basketmaker sites. Necklaces of juniper seeds evidently were extremely fashionable, strung alone or mixed with shell and stone. Most commonly they were worn in long strands looped one or more times around the neck. The nutlike pit was ground at both ends and a fiber cord was passed through the central cavity. They were then rolled between abrading stones to grind down the sides, sometimes until they attained a tubular appearance. Originally light brown in color, they darkened with wear until they became a lustrous black (Morris and Burgh 1954).

Wood, often painted, was used in the production of many types of jewelry: beads, pendants, ear tabs, and less common ornaments such as combs and nose plugs. Wooden pendants from U-Bar Cave were carved from yucca bloom stalk and painted a malachite greenish blue to imitate turquoise. Wood also often was used as a backing for mosaic.

Easily carved with stone implements, when wood was to be curved or bent it was made pliable by steaming. Joining was accomplished by the insertion of small wooden pegs, much as it sometimes is by contemporary Pueblo craftsmen. Holes sometimes were drilled to interlock separate pieces. A common method of repair was to drill holes on each side of a break, then tightly secure the two edges with rawhide lashings.

If we may judge by the attitudes of their modern descendants, to the prehistoric Indians, feathers had not merely an ornamental but a symbolic and ceremonial significance. Unfortunately, as in the case of vegetal remains, it is rare to find feathered articles intact other than when preserved under special circumstances, as in dry caves. However, our knowledge of how they were worn is enhanced by illustrations in ancient rock art, kiva murals, and even on pottery, all confirming the relation to present-day use. Bird bone usually is better preserved than feathers, and that helps to give us information as to what species were available in specific areas at specific times. Eagle feathers were without doubt among the most prized, but others were highly valued too, a few of the more common being turkey, hawk, quail, flicker, jay, raven, and duck.

For purposes of ornament, no feathers were more brilliant than those of the parrots and macaws who

Head of "arrow-swallower" showing feather adornment, from a Rio
Grande style petroglyph in the Galisteo Basin. From *Rock Art in
New Mexico*, by Polly Schaafsma.

inhabit Mexico and Central America. Their remains in the Southwest attest to the extensive trade which was carried on between these regions throughout most of the pre-Spanish era. Not only were feathers traded, but so were the live birds, which could be kept caged for periodic removal of the feathers, a practice which has persisted into modern times. Their importance to their prehistoric owners is reflected in the discovery of numerous parrot burials.

Feathers were attached to headdresses, combs, and pins or were worn in the hair; they also were tied in bunches to form pendants and dress ornaments. Necklaces were fashioned by bending the quills and lashing them with sinew, which was then attached to neck cords. Feathered bands adorned head, arms, and legs, and it is even likely that feathers were worn in ears and noses.

Bone was used almost interchangeably with shell and stone in the production of jewelry, and most of the items mentioned under these categories existed also in bone. Bone bracelets and rings, in fact, usually resembled those made of shell. Although the Hohokam and Mogollon did not utilize bone to the degree observed at Anasazi sites, it was employed by them to some extent. In addition to carved bone, a few examples of Hohokam painted bone and horn have been discovered, and still other finds may have lost all traces of pigment.

Excavation at Unshagi ruin (ca. 1375–1628) in the Jemez
Mountains, New Mexico, 1928–1934. Photo Archives,
Museum of New Mexico.

Among the Anasazi, animal and even occasionally human bone, horn, and antler all were extensively utilized for the manufacture of ornaments. Clearly, bone in its natural form required little modification to make attractive or unusual beads and pendants. Mandibles or scapulae could be drilled for suspension, as could teeth, claws, and horns. Leg bones of small mammals were made into tinklers. A necklace, belonging to the Laboratory of Anthropology, composed of fish vertebrae strung as beads, was recovered at Unshagi, an Anasazi ruin in the Jemez region. Illustrated in figure 34 is a neck ornament from the Rio Grande site of Pecos. It consists of a portion of a mammal rib, curved to fit the neck and drilled at each end so that it might be laced to form a choker or collar.

With a bit more effort, bone could be carved into bracelets, rings, pins, buttons, or dress ornaments. However, it was as beads and pendants, carved into all the usual pendant shapes, that it found its most common use. Basketmakers fabricated hemispherical bone beads resembling those made of stone.

But by far the most universal type of bone bead or pendant was tubular. It was formed simply by incising a segment of a bird or mammal long bone in two places, sawing with a sharp stone tool, and then breaking off the ends, leaving a tube of the desired length. The rough edges were usually finished by grinding. It could subsequently be strung through the hollow center and worn as a bead, either in a necklace or sewed to clothing. Alternatively, it could be grooved or perforated and worn as a drop pendant. A pendant might also be worn horizontally, strung through drilled perforations at each end. A variation of perforation was notched sides around which a cord could be tied. Bone tubes are found in sites of all cultures throughout the Southwest. Sometimes their purpose only can be inferred, since similar tubes were made into whistles or put to a variety of other uses. At times, when dealing with unperforated specimens, only the size, degree of finish on the ends, and possible decoration can serve as criteria for designating them as beads.

The most common methods for working bone, horn, and antler included cutting or sawing with a sharp stone implement; grinding, done on an abrasive stone sometimes grooved for shaping; and finally polishing. Polishers themselves were made of bone, among other materials. If bone or antler was to be bent, then steaming was probably the means by which this was accomplished.

In addition to bone, horn, and antler, many other types of animal remains were employed in the manufacture of adornment. Turtle shell, both durable and decorative, was one such material, especially suitable for making pendants and gorgets. In addition to claws and teeth strung with little modification, more elaborate ornaments were sometimes fashioned. At Aztec Ruin, for instance, a pendant made of beaver incisors carved and inlaid with turquoise was found.

Among the most readily obtainable materials for the manufacture of a wide assortment of articles was hair, both animal and human. Products ranged from tawny dog-hair belts to typical Basketmaker necklaces which incorporated lustrous dark brown human hair cordage.

Hide, too, was fashioned into necklaces, ranging from neck cords to leather disc beads. Still more exotic to modern tastes were the many bezoars used as ornaments at Hawikuh, which consisted of indurated masses of hair from the stomachs of deer. Often they were attached to, or in close association with, the mosaic-decorated combs discovered there.

The animal substance called lac, discussed earlier with regard to its use at Ridge Ruin as an adhesive, evidently also was employed as a modelling agent. One recovered ornament made entirely from lac is a bird attached to a broken shell bracelet, and other ornaments made partly from lac have been discovered.

ANASAZI ORNAMENTS

Evidence suggests that typical Basketmaker adornment included feather ornaments, frequently tied together as hair decorations; combs made from pointed wooden sticks, tied together and embellished with feathers and beads; ornaments of vegetal materials, especially seed beads; jewelry employing cordage, in particular necklaces of human hair; stone beads that were large and elongate or globular. (These last items gradually became less common as more shell was utilized.) Bone was generally scarce. Stone and shell mosaic pendants were introduced near the end of this era, probably from the Hohokam region. Necklaces were the most common form of Basketmaker adornment, especially a choker-type cord necklace with pendant beads attached exclusively to a short section of the front.

Feathers continued to be popular during the Pueblo I period. Stone beads, of a smaller size, were used more commonly; and there was a great increase in the incorporation of turquoise into jewelry of all kinds. By A.D. 900, stone carving and inlay constituted the most prominent ornamental techniques. Carved stone pendants often took the form of animals or birds. Some clay beads were manufactured. Disc beads were made both of stone and shell, and some pendants were made of animal remains. Glycymeris shell pendants and bracelets were popular. The end of the Developmental Period saw a great increase in the variety of ornament, including the use of copper bells.

The zenith of Anasazi culture occurred during what has been called Classic Pueblo. Minute beads were at their finest then, as were many forms of mosaics. Turquoise and shell were widely utilized. Pueblo IV, the last prehistoric period, saw the flowering of the Hopi, Zuni, and Rio Grande regions. Old forms of ornament were not rejected, but there were new influences and regional variations. Among the latter was a relative scarcity of beads in the Hopi district and the richness of mosaic at Hawikuh in the Zuni region. The Rio Grande area was characterized by abundant use of bone and antler; clay beads, pendants, and bells; and turquoise, shell, mica, and selenite.

HOHOKAM ORNAMENTS

Stone carving and mosaic were introduced during the Pioneer Stage, a time when there arose a preference for zoomorphic adornments. Turquoise predated shell in their construction. Shell bracelets and beads were popular in early phases. Shell carving had its beginnings at this time; the technique was passed on to the Anasazi and Mogollon, where it was similarly practiced except in the Rio Grande. During the Colonial Stage, stone carving became more elaborate, and flat animal shapes were typical. This stage was characterized by stone disc beads, turquoise inlaid on shell and stone, stone decorated by painting (rare), and a profusion of beautifully executed shell jewelry. Bone was much less commonly used at this time.

An influx of Mexican influences led to the Sedentary Stage. Earlier forms still were produced; but now they tended to become more ornate. Characteristic were quantities of copper bells; the new etched shell technique; the decline of stone carving, though it continued to be used in mosaics and in articles such as ear plugs and nose buttons, both typical Hohokam ornaments. During the final, Classic Stage of the River Hohokam, stone carving declined almost complete-

ly, although flat, wing-shaped schist pendants were extremely common.

At sites where Salado influence was predominant, there was outstanding stone carving, minute stone beads, and shell work, including ornaments with cut-out portions inlaid with pigment.

The Desert Branch of the Hohokam displayed differences based especially on differences of environment. Here there was more use of wood and vegetal materials, less of stone. Shell was popular in simpler forms.

MOGOLLON ORNAMENTS

Shell was the most important material in Mogollon jewelry, for which perishables, too, were widely used, especially in earlier periods. Later, ornaments of more durable substances were preferred. Shell bracelets and pendants have been found at most sites, becoming more complex with time. Many were carved in the Hohokam manner. Glycymeris bracelets developed from an early thin-edged form to one that was thick-edged and often decorated. Minute disc beads of shell, stone, and clay characterized later levels. The final flowering of the Mimbres Phase reflected both Anasazi and other influences. Shell, stone and bone rings, including figure-eight beads, were a late introduction, probably from the Hohokam, as were copper bells and some clay pendants.

Although Hohokam and Mogollon cultures had disappeared by the end of the fifteenth century, Pueblo peoples of the Hopi area, of western New Mexico, and of the Rio Grande Valley have preserved their traditions in dynamic vitality through the vast changes of succeeding centuries to the present day.

HISTORIC SOUTHWESTERN JEWELRY
1598 TO 1880

The conclusion of the Prehistoric Period coincided with settlement by the Spaniards and the beginning of written records. Thereafter, documents detailing jewelry and other articles brought into the

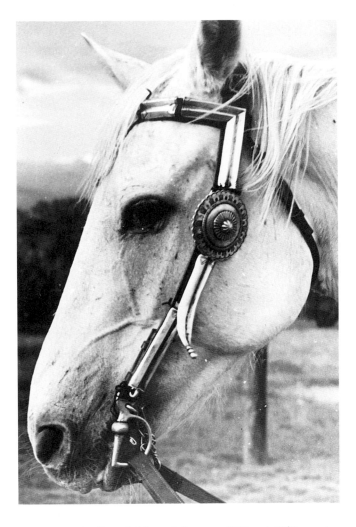

Navajo headstall, probably made between 1900 and 1940, reveals the Spanish influence on Native American styles and materials.

Southwest for trade supplemented discoveries of such items in excavated sites.

Juan de Oñate, who came to settle New Mexico in 1598, brought trade items, including glass beads of many varieties, glass earrings and buttons, rings of bone and jet, tin medals, hawksbells, and even Flemish mirrors.

As Spanish goods flowed into the Southwest, metal now was available in many manufactured forms: crosses, buttons, buckles, pendants, and various ornaments for horsegear. Silver, introduced by the Spaniards and worked locally by their silversmiths, became an especially important substance. In time, it would be worked by Indians. Another material

which became extremely popular after 1750 was Mediterranean coral.

Probably no more than a few centuries before the end of the Prehistoric Period, a new people had migrated into the Southwest: Athabascan speakers who were to become Navajos and Apaches. Like the indigenous Pueblos, they utilized local resources for ornamentation and continued to do so after the advent of the Spaniards. A Navajo pendant of coiled basketry, dating about 1700 to 1775, mirrors Navajo basketry technique exactly and still contains a fragment of handspun wool yarn used for suspension. The Navajos also introduced jewelry acquired from Europeans, either directly or through trade with the Plains Indians. Beads of shell, bone, and stone, and especially turquoise, continued to be popular but now had to compete with coral and glass beads and various metal ornaments acquired in trade.

After 1821, when Mexico won independence from Spain, American traders flocked into the Southwest. They, too, introduced unfamiliar trade goods. By 1846, at the time of the war between the United States and Mexico, Navajos were wearing bracelets of brass almost surely made by themselves from commercial brass wire obtained from these traders. True silver continued to be the most favored metal. German silver, an alloy of copper, zinc, and nickel common among Plains tribes in the 1800s, also found its way into the Southwest.

Perhaps in the 1850s, and certainly by the end of the 1860s, Navajos learned to work silver. Atsidi Sani, a smith who worked primarily with iron, generally is credited with being the first Navajo to make articles of silver, possibly having learned the craft from a Mexican smith as early as 1853. There is evidence that some, although probably very little, silver was worked during the Navajo internment at Bosque Redondo. By the end of 1869, with the return to their old territory, the Navajos had become fully accomplished silversmiths.

With the simplest of tools they made ornaments for themselves and their horses. Silver was hammered on anvils rigged from tree stumps, pieces of railroad tracks, or any suitable available surface. In making

Navajo jeweler, Pine Springs, Arizona, ca. 1920s. Photo Archives,
Museum of New Mexico.

objects of brass or copper wire only hammering to the desired shape was required. A silversmith had to master more complex techniques. Coins were the primary source of silver for early smiths. To make articles of any size, several coins were melted and cast into ingots, which then were hammered into sheet metal. To relieve internal stresses, the silver had first to be annealed, or tempered, by heating and then cooling rapidly. Hammering, bending, drawing of wire, and other processes were accomplished while the metal was cold.

In addition to fashioning jewelry from sheet silver, early smiths learned to cast pieces directly from molds carved to duplicate the desired design. The earliest molds were of wood, clay, or a fine-grained sandstone. Later they were made of tufa. Finished pieces were ground with stones or filed, then polished with sand or ashes and buffed with buckskin. A very early cast silver bracelet is illustrated in figure 65.

Tools used in the production of early silver were few and crude. Hammers, pliers, and tongs were basic. The cold chisel had a straight edge and was used for cutting before saws became readily available. Scissors also were employed to cut sheet metal. Early decoration was achieved by cutting into the metal with files (fig. 63) or with hammer and cold chisel (fig. 66); by graving or tracing a design with the sharp point of an awl or file; or by rocker engraving. Rocker engraving was done with a small tool having a chisellike edge that could be pushed forward and at the same time rocked from side to side, forming a zig-zag pattern (fig. 81). By about 1875 the technique had died out. File ends were used to punch dots and holes. Pipe stamps, made by smiths, produced circular or semicircular indentations hammered into the metal. This process in time led to the manufacture of full-fledged die stamps.

By 1880, the Navajo silversmith generally possessed a crude forge and goatskin bellows, an anvil of any suitable bit of available iron, and a crucible made perhaps of clay or iron pipe sealed at one end. Molds still were much as previously described. The difficult technique of soldering was now in its infancy and soon would be mastered.

A very important early smith working in the 1870s was named Atsidi Chon. He has been credited with making the first silver headstall for horses (fig. 81) and the first concha belt. The concha was probably adopted by Navajos from a Mexican prototype. However, stringing them on a belt is a fashion which may have been inspired by the German silver, disc-shaped hair plates worn strung together by Plains Indian men and, sometimes, as belts by Plains women. A belt with Plains-style, undecorated German silver conchas is illustrated in figure 62. Such pieces were rare in the Southwest. The one shown here belonged to Manuelito, a famous Navajo war chief.

As first designed by Navajo smiths, conchas were round or oval. They had scalloped edges and the rims were usually decorated with a pattern of alternating parallel lines and punched holes or dots. Centers were cut out by cold chisel in the form of opposed triangles with a solid bar between—a cut-out diamond—over which a belt could be laced. At first, the area between this center and the outer zone was left plain (fig. 118). Later, stamped designs were added.

Silver-decorated horse gear was of Spanish derivation, perhaps by way of the southern Plains. It included conchas and buttons as well as plates to decorate forehead and cheek straps. The latter sometimes terminated in tiny handlike elements (fig. 81).

The Navajo *najahe*, a single or double crescent-shaped ornament cut from sheet metal or cast, originated in North Africa as a bridal ornament before crossing to Spain and eventually to the New World. Here, too, it was an ornament for horses before being hung from silver necklaces for decorative purposes. Sometimes the ends of the crescent were shaped into tiny hands. These often are called "hands of Fatima" (recalling their old North African origins), but they are called *chee*, or grandfather, hands by Navajos. *Chee* hands were not limited to *najahes* but appeared on such articles as bangle bracelets (fig. 64).

Manuelito, Navajo War Chief, 1874. Photograph by Ben Wittick. Photo Archives, Museum of New Mexico.

79

Navajo silversmith, Gallup, New Mexico, ca. 1930. Arranged around him are the design stamps, pliers, snips, and railroad-rail anvil of his trade. To his left is a simple forge for melting silver into ingots, which will be used in manufacturing jewelry.
Photo Archives, Museum of New Mexico.

Buttons were made from hammered silver coins domed by forcing them into a curved depression. At first, two holes were punched in the center for attachment. But, as soldering was learned, buttons were provided with small loops on the backs.

The earliest silver beads also were domed hemispheres. Later, two were soldered together to produce a hollow, globular bead. Necklaces of silver beads with *najahe* pendants were later decorated with what are commonly known as squash blossoms. These derived from Spanish silver trouser ornaments known as pomegranate blossoms. Like the latter, early petals were usually relatively short; they grew longer with time.

Other ornaments made in those early years included manta pins, earrings, rings, bracelets, and wrist guards, called by the Navajos *ketohs*. Manta pins—sharpened silver prongs with ornamental heads—were used to fasten Navajo woven dresses at the shoulders. They disappeared when mantas themselves ceased to be worn.

Many of the earlier earrings had been made of turquoise. In historic times turquoise was supplanted by silver, copper, or such materials as glass trade beads. Early metal earrings were simple wire loops on which one or two sliding silver beads were later strung. It has been said that Navajo men formerly wore this style of earring, changing back to turquoise when it became plentiful, and that the opposite was true for women, who turned from loops of shell, glass beads, and turquoise to metal loops. Women, in fact, did not wear earrings as frequently as did men. Photographs taken at Bosque Redondo tend to bear out these preferences. The change in materials and styles for both sexes—again, on photographic evidence—appears to have begun to take place around the 1880s.

The very early bracelet seen in figure 63 probably was made from a brass ramrod. Most early metal bracelets were simple file-decorated silver or brass wire bangles. Wire was obtained from traders, then it was hammered or drawn by Navajo smiths themselves, and eventually, in the twentieth century, it was obtained commercially in several styles: carinated, twisted, round, and square (fig. 119). Navajo smiths also produced band bracelets hammered from sheet metal or sometimes cast. Rings usually were hammered solid bands, but occasionally were cast. So, too, were *ketohs*. Backings, such as leather, often were decorated with bone or shell and later with European copper and brass. Such materials continued in use until Navajos learned to work silver. They then began to fashion silver plates to adorn these useful articles.

In 1872, Atsidi Chon stayed for a time at Zuni Pueblo, visiting a friend, Lanyade, destined himself to become a famous smith. Zunis already were blacksmiths and knew how to work copper and brass. Lanyade now learned silverworking, most probably from Chon, and taught the skill to other Zunis.

Among Hopis of the period, jewelry was little favored, and no metal ornaments were made by Hopis themselves. However, silver jewelry was produced at Acoma in the 1870s, and it was traded from there to nearby Laguna, where a few smiths also made silver jewelry. The craft was not represented by Pueblo smiths in the Rio Grande area at this time except for some silver made as Isleta, brought there by a few migrating Laguna smiths in 1879.

Nineteenth-century Apache metalwork was primarily in iron and also in brass. With the exception of a few trade items, their adornment on the whole resembled that of Plains tribes more than that of either Navajos or Pueblos. Apaches made brass studs to decorate belts and saddles. Their concha belts were wide leather bands adorned with large, undecorated, Plains-style brass discs, and they also favored wide, heavy brass bracelets. Strings of shell were prized. Glass trade beads commonly were used as ornaments, especially in bead necklaces and ear pendants. Beadwork was, and is, an important Apache craft, applied to a wide range of articles.

Navajo jeweler at Gallup Ceremonial, New Mexico, 1920–1940.
Photo Archives, Museum of New Mexico.

Navajo jeweler, Pine Springs, Arizona. Photo Archives,
Museum of New Mexico.

SOUTHWESTERN JEWELRY,
1880 TO 1960

Among Navajos and Pueblos alike, the love of turquoise, coral, and shell continued strong, despite the introduction of metal ornaments (fig. 112). Necklaces appearing around the turn of the century demonstrate the transition of the *jokla* pendant (loops of shell, glass, or stone, primarily turquoise, beads) from an ear ornament to a pendant hung from a necklace.

In the 1880s Hopis had begun to wear Zuni-made silver ornaments, and these became more widespread in the following decade. In 1898, the Zuni smith Lanyade visited a friend, Sikyatala, at Sichomovi, First Mesa. Sikyatala thereafter became the first Hopi silversmith, and it was he who taught the craft to other Hopis. However, it was not until much later that the working of silver became as important as at Zuni and a distinctive Hopi style emerged and flourished.

The years between 1880 and 1900 have been called the classic period of Navajo and Pueblo silverwork. New tools and techniques came into use, and a greater refinement of the art produced fine articles that successfully reflected the tastes and needs of the people who created them. With the mastery of soldering, for example, composite objects could be created. A coin soldered to a silver band represented a means of embellishment devised before Navajos learned the setting of stones. Soldering made possible also the later use of appliqué decoration —small curled elements of wire (fig. 126), tiny silver drops often called teardrops or raindrops, and decorated plates or plaques added to items such as bracelets or rings (fig. 142).

Soldering was a complicated process for smiths working with quite simple tools and materials, who manufactured the solder from silver and brass filings. It was placed in the joint to be sealed, along with a flux made from aluminum sulphate garnered from the surrounding countryside (borax eventually was substituted). The objects to be joined, fastened together with fine iron wire, were laid on the coals of a forge. Cotton rags soaked in mutton fat or some similar grease fed the fire, while a more intense heat was obtained with the aid of a handmade blowpipe. In later years, the blowtorch and commercial solder made the process considerably easier.

This period witnessed the growth of a vital component of Navajo silverworking, the fabrication of stamps that could be used to transfer whole design elements. It grew from the development of the simple pipe stamp and, ultimately, was derived from tooling done by Mexican leather workers. Great skill was required to carve a relief pattern onto a tiny scrap of steel, utilizing file and chisel to remove parts of the surface in order to form a relief design. This was a positive die, used to impress the design into silver or to make a negative die by pressing the heated steel into a blank metal cylinder.

Two other techniques by which relief decoration was applied to flat surfaces now came into use. Repoussé, which was in wide use by the 1890s and continued very popular well into the twentieth century, refers to a free hand design produced by hammering from the back of the object. Relief was heightened by stamping on the front, around the edges of the image. Embossing also involved striking a pattern from the reverse, in this case using a specific stamp, most often spherical.

Finally, it was during this period that the setting of stones in silver was begun, a laborious, trial-and-error process. The technique differed from inlay or overlay in that it involved gripping the stone in a strip of silver—a bezel—which was then soldered to its foundation. Early bezels were large and tended to overlap the usually small, flat stone. Around the turn of the century, bezels grew thinner. Stones were hand cut and hand polished. Turquoise undoubtedly was the favored material, but at this time it was scarce and any likely available substance might be employed, from crudely cut native garnets to bits of glass. The cast bracelet illustrated in figure 65 is set with native garnets. The bracelet, thought to date from the late 1870s, represents one of the earliest examples of a stone set in silver.

Navajo silversmiths also turned their considerable talents to the manufacture of utilitarian items. Miniature silver canteens, used as tobacco or powder flasks, probably were derived from Mexican prototypes. They made objects such as silver powder measures, bells, and tweezers, also for their own use.

Silver articles made at this time by Pueblo smiths still tended to resemble those of Navajos. But when, in the 1890s, the Zunis learned to set stones, a marked stylistic difference soon developed. It arose from a basic difference in viewpoint. To Navajos, stones were of secondary interest to the silverwork they adorned. Zunis, superb lapidaries since prehistoric times and with a deep religious attachment to turquoise, came to regard silver primarily as a background for elaborate settings. The years after 1900 saw the rapid development among the Pueblos of this approach.

The use of silver crosses on necklaces of silver and coral beads was characteristic of Pueblo smiths—especially at Acoma, Laguna, and Isleta. These might be tiny crosses within the necklace itself or larger crosses that often served as pendants. Among the latter was a double-barred form resembling the cross of Lorraine, perhaps reflecting a mixture of Christian symbolism with Pueblo tradition, which regarded it as the dragonfly, a water symbol. Frequently this type of cross featured a heart-shaped terminal with one concave edge. It is called an "indented," "bruised," or "lazy" heart.

During the 1880s, railroads reached the Southwest, harbingers of a tourist market that was to affect profoundly the future of Indian silverwork. The influence of scattered white traders who had reached the Navajo reservation in the 1870s was overshadowed in the early 1900s by commercial enterprises centered in cities such as Albuquerque, Gallup, and Flagstaff. In the 1890s, commercially refined, one-ounce slugs of silver had replaced coins formerly used by Navajo smiths (to be supplanted in time by commercial sheet silver). Around the turn of the century, Herman Schweizer, head of the curio department of the Fred Harvey Company, began to furnish specific amounts of silver and precut turquoise to be made up into light-. weight jewelry for the tourist trade. The years between 1900 and 1940 were marked by a proliferation of hastily manufactured curios displaying nontraditional designs: thunderbirds, swastikas, and arrows (fig. 98). Superior craftsmanship, however, did not die. And the availability of new and better tools and materials encouraged continued experimentation. Some non-Indian forms made for sale included, besides the cheap baubles, an array of finely crafted objects exemplified by a comb (fig. 99), hairpins (fig. 162), and napkin rings.

As early as the 1880s, with the mastery of soldering, Navajo smiths had begun to make conchas with closed centers and a loop, usually copper, soldered to the back for stringing. Although no longer open, the diamond-shaped center frequently was retained as a focus for the increasingly ornate repoussé and stamped designs radiating from it. By the 1920s, the practice of setting turquoise in conchas had become prevalent (fig. 118). Also dating from the twentieth century were butterfly-shaped plaques strung between conchas.

Headstalls, too, grew more elaborate and after 1900 were ornamented with turquoise (fig. 105) as were *ketohs*. Heavy wrought-silver wrist guards were decorated by stamping and repoussage (figs. 106, 107), while cast specimens achieved a more delicate elegance (fig. 161). In a notable study of traditional southwestern Indian silverwork, H. P. Mera wrote that the *ketoh* illustrated in figure 108 represented "a peak in the art of casting in stone molds" (Mera 1959). Since mid-century, production of *ketohs* has declined markedly.

Other items that continued to be made by Navajo smiths primarily for Indian use included dress and collar ornaments (fig. 143), hat bands, buttons, and silver-decorated medicine pouches (fig. 165).

Early in the twentieth century, Navajo bracelets began to display multiple settings, matched and sometimes graduated. For about a decade, in the 1920s, cabochon cut stones became fashionable—a domed style that contrasted with the earlier flat type and that enjoyed a revival after 1940 (fig. 120). There were band bracelets and bar bracelets, and carinated bars, triangular in cross-section, were very popular. So were bracelets composed of multiple bars or wires, splayed to support their diverse settings. Wire appliqué grew more elaborate (fig. 138). In the 1930s, bead wire, resembling a row of teardrops, was especially prevalent. Also during the 1930s and 1940s, huge stones were used to embellish bracelets and rings (fig. 138).

In the 1930s, row work, in particular the setting of turquoise in clusters (originally a Navajo style), came to be regarded as characteristically Zuni. It was entirely in keeping with the Zuni predilection for covering silver with turquoise or other stones. Turquoise clusters decorated bracelets (figs. 121, 122), rings, and earrings. In row work, each small stone is set in its individual bezel. The ancient technique of mosaic, carried into the twentieth century, involved setting stones side by side. One type is the checkerboard mosaic ring in figure 157.

Jewelry making became an important economic activity at Zuni during the 1930s, practiced by both men and women. The first and one of the most celebrated of Zuni women smiths was Della Casi.

After the turn of the century both Zuni and Navajo rings were set with larger stones than the early, small, single, central stone that characterized the first settings. To support them, the solid silver band was replaced by a band with split splayed ends.

Earrings, too, changed form. Silver loops were replaced by cone-shaped silver drops and still later by turquoise-decorated silver pendants, many of which, Navajo and Pueblo alike, became more elaborate under Zuni influence (fig. 126). Bead loops or

A fine example of shell set in silver is seen in this Pueblo pendant, made in the 1920s. The hand has nacreous shell fingernails and an inlaid turquoise ring. (Detail, plate 123.)

joklas were relegated to the bottom of necklaces.

Necklaces came in many varieties. The squash blossom style grew more showy (fig. 125) and *najahes* more complex. A popular style of the 1920s to 1930s featured two strands of small silver beads, each strand threaded through the elongated shanks of silver squash blossoms (fig. 124).

In addition to silver necklaces, stone, shell, jet, and coral retained their desirability (fig. 136). Strands of turquoise disc beads might be mingled with necklaces of coral and shell. Very small brown-white shell disc beads called *heishi,* sometimes strung between other beads, were worn alone in single or multiple strands. The necklaces pictured in figure 139 mix coral with beads of silver.

A unique example of inlay on shell is the hand illustrated in figure 123 with its mother of pearl nails

and slender turquoise ring. Puebloan mosaic on shell or bone backings was another prehistoric technique that endured into the twentieth century. An especially fine example of turquoise mosaic on bone may be seen in the necklace in figure 137. Most common was the bivalve shell pendant decorated with turquoise, coral, jet, and white shell. Toward the end of the tourist period, around the mid 1940s, necklaces copying this style were manufactured primarily at Santo Domingo Pueblo, using scraps of low grade or imitation turquoise, plastic "coral," and broken bits of phonograph record in place of jet (these now have become collector's items). By this time, concern over the flood of cheap, poorly crafted tourist jewelry that had come to dominate the market led to the establishment of a number of programs aimed at encouraging traditional designs and techniques, establishing standards, developing markets, and improving the status of smiths. A pioneer in this effort was the Indian Arts and Crafts Board. Following World War II, craft guilds proliferated. With the assistance of the GI bill, a number of young smiths received training through various public and private programs that employed master silversmiths as teachers.

In 1941, Ambrose Roanhorse, who had taught at the Santa Fe Indian School and had worked with the Laboratory of Anthropology's Kenneth Chapman, became director of the Navajo Arts and Crafts Enterprise. One of the most important artists of the period, Navajo Kenneth Begay, is represented by the unique silver belt seen in figure 160.

Special encouragement was given to Hopi smiths by the Museum of Northern Arizona. Although it had its beginnings in the late 1930s, Hopi overlay became widespread following the war. This technique involved soldering one silver band with cut-out design upon a second band that provided an oxidized background. Although its popularity has led to the use of the technique by other tribes, overlay remains chiefly identified with the Hopis. The silver-on-silver belt buckle seen in figure 163 was made by one of Ambrose Roanhorse's pupils, Louis Lomay, a well-known Hopi silversmith.

Another technique which flourished after 1940,

Zuni silversmiths, 1936. Photo Archives, Museum of New Mexico.

although it may have been devised as far back as 1929, was Zuni channel work. In this style, stones are cemented into a series of small silver "boxes" formed by soldering the individual sides of each compartment at right angles to the base.

At the Santa Fe Indian School, metalwork was introduced to students from many tribal backgrounds. From this time on, silverworkers were to be found among Apaches (fig. 159), as well as in pueblos such as Cochiti (figs. 118, 168) and Santo Domingo (fig. 164). A generation of talented young newcomers was emerging alongside the older masters.

CONTEMPORARY SOUTHWESTERN JEWELRY, 1960S TO 1980S

The 1960s heralded a new era in southwestern arts, spurred by a sudden worldwide enthusiasm for all things Indian. Prices soared, with mixed results.

Again, a flood of mass-produced articles and imitation "Indian" jewelry was competing with traditionally crafted pieces as they still do. Machine casting (centrifugal and spin casting), for example, utilizes a rubber mold of a handmade original from which numerous wax duplicates can be made. These, connected to wax ducts and surrounded by plaster within a metal container, are heated to melt away the wax. As the container is spun on a motor driven arm, silver is pumped into the now-empty spaces within the plaster by centrifugal force. The finished result is a quantity of cast ornaments that, at first glance, very much resemble the original. Besides hand cast jewelry, Hopi overlay is frequently imitated by spin casting.

Turquoise, now almost always machine cut and polished, has long been imitated when the real thing was unavailable or too costly. The painted wooden pendants from U-Bar Cave, previously described, are examples of imitations that created items rarer in this century than if they *had* been made of turquoise. Today, stones similar to turquoise may be set in silver or low-grade turquoise may be stabilized—and sometimes improved—through impregnation with plastics. Silver may be inlaid with fragments of turquoise and coral, a process called fragment inlay. This is not Zuni inlay but a frugal technique practiced by Navajos.

The recent popularity of Indian jewelry is not confined to tourists. It is sought after also by collectors, and the consequently higher prices have encouraged serious craftspeople to expend the time and effort necessary to create jewelry of outstanding workmanship. Creative young artists have been inspired to compete and win awards in craft shows throughout the United States.

Some of the more recently developed techniques include appliqué on an oxidized background, which evolved into shadowbox, with its incurled rim and domed overlay. A related style, pedestal overlay, highlights a cut-out figure mounted above a slightly concave, stippled, oxidized backing. Wrought flanged or "stacked" silver (fig. 178) features thin silver plates set on edge, side by side. Old techniques, too, survive in contemporary variations. The fluted silver beads in figure 179 are not greatly different from early examples.

Materials of every description are used in contemporary Indian jewelry. Many-colored shells are carved into "fetish" necklaces at Santo Domingo and especially at Zuni, where they reflect a tradition of finely carved stone birds and animals (fig. 175). Turquoise and other stones obtained from far-distant countries are set into silver, gold, and brass. Santo Domingo can boast several families of excellent lapidaries, producing exceptional turquoise beads.

At Zuni, row work has grown increasingly more delicate. Highly popular is the style called petit point, a phrase that covers a multitude of tiny shapes: teardrop, oval, round, triangular, and even needlepoint, which is an elongate, slender stone pointed at both ends.

Motifs now are drawn from many and varied

sources, most rooted in native traditions. A very contemporary necklace, illustrated in figure 177, combines stones of disparate origins with a silver pendant and clasps decorated by Mimbres bat designs. Innovation flourishes today, yet traditional values still remain at the heart of the contemporary jeweler's craft.

Navajo girl waiting to enter competition of clothing contest at Indian Market, Santa Fe, New Mexico, ca. 1960s. Photograph courtesy Southwestern Association on Indian Affairs.

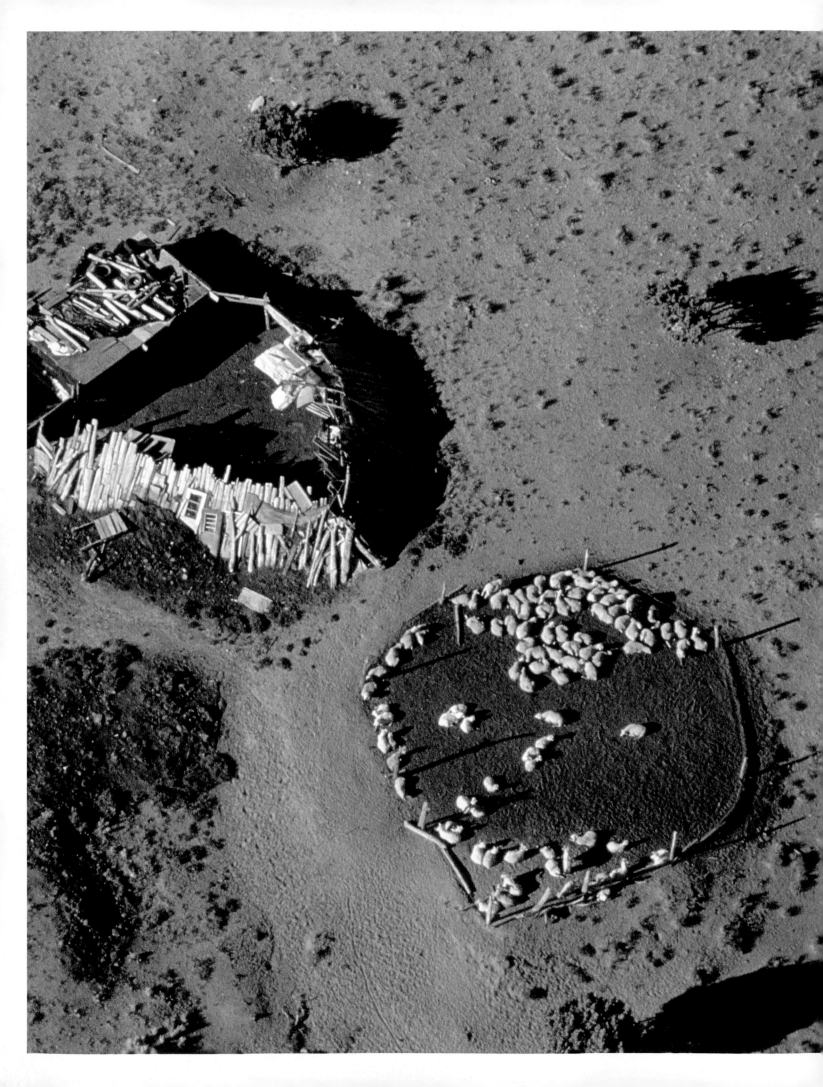

THE HISTORY OF
SOUTHWESTERN WEAVING

KATE PECK KENT

Navajo Sheep and Corrals, Marsh Pass, Arizona.
Photograph by Paul Logsdon.

TEXTILE PRODUCTION CAN BE TRACED through the archaeological record back in time to about A.D. 200 in the San Juan River drainage, that area we call the Four Corners, where the modern states of Utah, Colorado, New Mexico, and Arizona meet. Here, between A.D. 200 and 700, Basketmaker cultures flourished, and the people left evidence of their fiber skills in rock shelters and caves where, protected from the elements, the textiles lay hidden until discovered by twentieth-century archaeologists. Very similar remains, roughly contemporaneous to those of the Basketmakers, have also been found in southern and southwestern New Mexico.

The ancient people utilized a wide variety of plant fibers for their textiles, most especially fibers from the leaves of yucca plants or the stems of apocynum (Indian hemp) and milkweed (Asclepius). These

Pueblo III (1100–pre-1300) cotton textile fragment of diagonal twill weave with black, red, and white stripes. Found at Canyon de Chelly, Arizona. Photo Archives, Museum of New Mexico.

were twisted into yarn probably without the aid of a spindle but by rolling them between the thigh and palm of the hand in accordance with a simple process almost universally used for such materials. Human hair was twisted into sturdy cordage. Hair or wool of various animals was utilized also. Among examples that have been preserved are braided sashes made from dog hair yarn, a band of buffalo hair yarn, and one belt reportedly of rabbit fur yarn. Warm pile cord was made by twisting bear, deer, rabbit fur, and bird down between the plies of yucca cordage. The most usual use of rabbit skins and those of other small animals and even birds was to cut a skin in strips and wrap it about fiber cordage to make lengths of fur cord. Toward the end of Basketmaker times feather cord, made by wrapping turkey feathers on yucca yarn, began to replace fur cord.

These various kinds of yarn and cordage were fashioned into articles of clothing and utilitarian household goods. Soft, warm blankets were made for infants and adults alike from the fur and later feather cord. Sturdy yucca yarn served in the manufacture of sandals, which vary in style and technique throughout the Basketmaker and later periods (fig. 13). The sole of sandals of this type is worked in a geometric pattern of small knots, while the inner surface, which fits against the foot, bears a totally different, sometimes quite complex tapestry weave design in colored wefts (photo, right). The inner and outer surfaces of the sandal sole were woven simultaneously on a single set of structural warps, not made separately and then sewn together. It is possible that the knotting on the underside would furnish traction on wet surfaces, or that the pattern, pressed in sand, would serve to identify its wearer. In any event it seems remarkable that so much time, effort, and skill were expended in weaving designs which would not show when the sandals were worn.

Geometric patterns like those on the sandals are found on tapestry-woven women's apron fronts, tumplines, cradle bands, twined bags, and coiled baskets. A tumpline, or carrying band, is a narrow band ten or twelve inches long with a loop at each end. The band is placed about the forehead. Ropes running

Prehistoric Basketmaker sandals, tumpline, fashioned of sturdy
yucca yarn. Photo Archives, Museum of New Mexico.

through the loops are tied to a load on the shoulders or back, thus helping to support it. Warps of a tumpline must be strong enough not to break under tension and are usually of very heavy yucca twine, or sometimes sturdy hair cord. Wefts are woven tightly over these cords so as to completely cover them. The weft material is soft—apocynum or fine yucca yarn designed to be comfortable against the wearer's skin. When cotton fiber, brought by trade from southern Arizona and New Mexico, reached the Four Corners area after A.D. 600, one finds it used as weft in tumplines and cradle bands alike. (A cradle band is somewhat wider than a tumpline. Its ends were fastened to the edges of a baby's cradle and kept the infant securely in place.) The use of cotton for wefts in tump-

lines becomes increasingly common in the Southwest after Basketmaker times.

Yucca and apocynum yarns were used also for the manufacture of soft twined-weft bags of all sizes. Some of these were large enough to serve as burial shrouds for adults, split open and then sewed around the flexed body. Other bags, socks, and leggings were made by a process called looping in which a single long cord is looped on itself to give the effect of knitting. Yucca and human hair cord were fashioned into hunting nets and snares.

The Basketmakers and their contemporaries in southern New Mexico fabricated their textiles without the use of a loom with heddles for controlling warp sets. The nonloom finger processes they developed continued in use among the prehistoric Southwesterners after A.D. 700 with few changes. Cotton yarns were added to wild plant and animal fibers, and turkey feather blankets replaced the earlier fur cord wraps, but techniques of manufacture remained the same. For example, a looped sock from twelfth-century Chaco Canyon continued the tradition established centuries earlier by Basketmakers.

The large hunting net and looped pipe bag from U-Bar Cave in the New Mexico panhandle also demonstrate this carry-over from very early times (figs. 38, 41). They date to the late fourteenth century A.D. but are virtually identical to nets and bags made more than one thousand years before in northeastern Arizona. The U-Bar Cave net measures 151 feet long by 5 feet wide and is made of human hair twine. An

Human hair hunting net, 1200–1400, *in situ* at U-Bar Cave in southwestern New Mexico. *See also* figure 41.
Courtesy Laboratory of Anthropology.

estimated sixty-nine full heads of hair were required to produce the 1.54 miles of cordage used in the net. The piece was definitely the result of a community effort, not only in terms of the number of people who contributed their hair, but also because the manufacture of that amount of cordage would have required the time and effort of a good many artisans. It was found neatly folded and cached in a pit specially dug to hold it and lined with grass. Thirty snares accompanied it, and these and other artifacts indicate the cave was a ceremonial hunting shrine.

Nets of this kind were used into modern times in the Southwest for the communal hunting of rabbits. The net was stretched out like an extra-long tennis net and propped up with forked sticks. The ends were brought in to form an open V or crescent. The people spread out in a large semicircle, beating the grass ahead of them and driving rabbits against the net, where they were trapped and could be killed.

While the Basketmaker tradition of textile manufacture was maintained into historic times in the Southwest, it was enriched after A.D. 900 by a second tradition, loom weaving in cotton, introduced through trade with southern Arizona and northern Mexico. By about A.D. 1000 or 1100 cotton was grown as far north into Utah as the climate allowed and beautiful textiles in a number of complex techniques were woven on both the wide, upright loom and the backstrap loom. Cotton weaving in the Southwest was the most northerly manifestation of an indigenous art which flowered from Utah south through the Valley of Mexico and Central America to northern Chile long before Europeans reached the New World.

Protected archaeological sites such as the cliff dwellings of Mesa Verde, White House, Montezuma Castle, Tonto Monument, and the Upper Gila River drainage have yielded many examples of prehistoric cotton cloth—mantas, shirts, breechclouts, kilts, sashes, belts, bags, quivers, and other items, some exquisitely patterned. (Mantas are blankets woven wider than long and used as wrap-around dresses by women and shoulder robes by both sexes.)

A good idea of the variety, beauty, and form of

Repairing north kiva of Balcony House, Mesa Verde, Colorado, ca.
1910. Photograph by Jesse Nusbaum. Photo Archives,
Museum of New Mexico.

prehistoric cotton textiles can be gained from study-ing fifteenth-century kiva murals of ceremonial cos-tuming from the Hopi country and Pottery Mound and Kuaua near Albuquerque. Female dancers are depicted dressed in wrap-around manta dresses, fas-tened on one shoulder and held at the waist by a sash. Some of the black dresses are patterned by what were probably resist dye motifs. (In resist dyeing, portions of the fabric are protected from the dye bath, form-ing a pattern.) Male dancers wear kilts with borders decorated by geometric motifs, sashes, belts, and sometimes short shoulder blankets.

Spaniards, arriving in the Southwest in the six-teenth century, described textiles like those found pre-historically. So rich in fabrics were the Pueblo villagers of the time that they presented the newcomers with gifts of hundreds of blankets.

EARLY HISTORIC TEXTILES,
1598 TO 1880

The Pueblos carried on their traditional weaving after the Spanish colonists settled in the northern Rio

Grande Valley in 1598. Indeed, in the seventeenth century the Spaniards, before they had established their own weaving industry on European-style horizontal treadle looms, filled their textile needs by exploiting the Pueblos, demanding annual tribute in mantas.

While the Pueblos did not change the forms of the textiles they wove, maintaining their own costume styles, the Spanish presence did modify their work in some ways. The most apparent effect was the introduction of new materials. Sheep, brought from Mexico by the Spaniards, were added to the Pueblo economy well before A.D. 1650, and wool, spun on the same stick and whorl spindle used for cotton, was utilized immediately in Pueblo weavings. Indigo dye, another Mexican import, was also taken over in the seventeenth century. By 1700, for example, the woman's black manta dress illustrated in the Pottery Mound murals was woven of wool rather than cotton, with diamond twill weave borders in indigo blue, a format maintained until the present time. After trade cloth was made available the Pueblos raveled some of it to get red embroidery yarns, and in the nineteenth century commercial yarns were supplied by Spaniards and Americans, further modifying the appearance of Pueblo textiles.

There was the loss, probably shortly after the Spaniards arrived, of many complex weaving techniques and design systems common in prehistoric textiles. Painting of blankets was replaced by embroidery, the decoration confined to borders rather than covering the entire surface of the piece. The Spaniards did contribute the new skills of knitting and crochet, which replaced the earlier techniques of looping and braiding for socks and shirts. They also introduced a new blanket or serape shape, longer than wide like our bed blankets, rather than wider than long like the traditional Pueblo manta (fig. 50). These serapes were patterned by simple weft stripes. One style, probably introduced from Mexico in the 1600s, came to be known as the "Moqui pattern," which consists of narrow stripes in indigo blue, brown, and white. The term *Moqui* is an old word for Hopi and was applied

Navajo girls interned at the military reservation of Bosque Redondo in eastern New Mexico, 1864–1868. They are wearing the "Moqui" style patterned blankets. Note, also, their jewelry. This includes long, bead-loop earrings (probably shell and turquoise), several strings of beads made of shell and silver, and, on the woman at right, what appears to be a strand of slender coral tubes. The girl on the left has a pendant, possibly of inlaid shell, and wears a sleigh bell tied to one end of her belt. Photo Archives, Museum of New Mexico.

to this design by twentieth-century traders who erroneously thought such serapes were produced only, or principally, by that Pueblo group. In point of fact Moqui pattern blankets were made by the Spaniards on their treadle looms and by Pueblos and Navajos on the vertical loom throughout the early historic period.

Embroidery patterns on Pueblo mantas are a direct link to the past. The same motifs and design concepts seen in historic embroideries are found in woven and painted textiles from many prehistoric sites and are depicted on costumes in the fifteenth-century murals.

One characteristic of Pueblo decorative textile art is the use of "negative" design (fig. 57), clearly evident in the black borders of the white cotton manta wherein the pattern is made by white lines of ground cloth not covered by embroidery yarns. While negative patterning is seen in prehistoric textiles from most southwestern sites, it is an especially prominent feature of textile design among the Pueblo III (A.D. 1100 to 1300) Anasazi of northeastern Arizona and is found in black and white pottery of that period from the Kayenta area. The concept may relate to the resist dyeing of fabrics.

Stressing diagonal rather than vertical lines lends a dynamic quality to design. This is one characteristic of much Pueblo textile patterning. The hooks along the inner edge of the upper border on the white cotton manta, for example, are slanted to carry the eye from one side of the border to the other.

Finally, many of the motifs in historic embroideries may be matched in prehistoric textiles. Thus the two large diamond-shaped figures at the center of the white manta just below the upper border are found on textile fragments from twelfth-century southwestern New Mexico worked in a technique called weft-wrap openwork. Similar motifs are painted on Mimbres pottery from that area. These figures are generally spoken of as birds.

The only embroidery motifs one does not find in prehistoric southwestern textiles are certain floral figures taken from the Spanish in historic times. One of these, a double flower, may be seen repeated along the inner edges of the borders on some examples of the black Acoma mantas. A single flower was used by Zuni artisans and is thus asymmetrical.

A distinctive style of manta-dress developed at Zuni in the mid-nineteenth century (fig. 58). This was black wool diagonal twill weave like the woman's dress used in other Pueblos, but borders instead

of diamond twill in indigo blue wefts were embroidered with indigo blue yarns. There are some four geometric patterns used in this Zuni embroidery, the most common being stylized swallow tail butterflies, placed alternately head up, head down.

Another link with the past is the white manta with red and indigo blue borders which has been worn as a shoulder robe by women in historic times and is sometimes folded over and used as a kilt by a male dancer (fig. 147). These are woven in diagonal twill with diamond twill indigo blue borders. I believe they are modern versions of the twill weave cotton blankets, striped in red, white, and brown or black, fragments of which are found in almost every Pueblo III Anasazi site where textiles have survived. A diamond twill pattern often appears in the dark brown or black bands, which are analogous to the dark indigo bands of historic pieces.

Plaid patterned shoulder blankets are spoken of as traditional garments for men and boys among the Hopi. A few are still made for small boys, but apparently men turned to wearing Moqui pattern and other serapes by 1880 or earlier. Some handsome adult-size plaid blankets were produced during a revival of Hopi weaving sparked by the Museum of Northern Arizona in the 1930s and 1940s (fig. 152). Plaid textile fragments are found in fourteenth-century archaeological sites in central and southern Arizona, and plaids in a number of complex twilling techniques were prominent among textile fragments from the early eighteenth-century Hopi village of Walpi. This type of textile was certainly a part of the prehistoric weaving tradition inherited by the Hopi.

In studying the history of Pueblo weaving one is struck by the role tradition has played in stabilizing the forms, techniques, and design of their textiles. While Pueblo weavers at Hopi and Zuni did weave blankets for tourist sale in the latter half of the nineteenth century, Pueblo weaving remained centered on the production of traditional articles of clothing as it had before European intervention.

Athabascan-speaking Indians began to filter into the Southwest around A.D. 1500. Those who first con-

Acoma Embroidered Wool Manta, 1870–1880. The floral motif
along the inner edges of the borders is taken from the Spanish.

tacted the Pueblos of northern New Mexico came to
be called Navajos. These people were essentially
nomadic hunters and gatherers when they arrived, but
they soon learned from the Pueblos to cultivate crops
and after the Spaniards brought sheep undertook the
seminomadic life of pastoralists. By about A.D. 1650
Navajo women had learned the art of weaving from
Pueblos. For more than a century the products of their
looms were probably identical to those of their Pueblo teachers, consisting of the same kinds of clothing
as well as Spanish-style serapes. It was probably the
latter which became important trade articles as early
as 1700. Many may have been of the style called
Moqui pattern. The most common type of blanket,
used for everyday wear, was striped brown and white.

By the end of the 1700s Navajo weaving had
begun to diverge from traditional Pueblo styles in a
number of ways. The one-piece wrap-around manta-
dress, which was worn by both Navajo and Pueblo
women, was discarded in favor of a two-piece blanket dress, front and back sections being fastened over
both shoulders, sewed together up the sides and belt-
ed at the waist (fig. 71).

The designs on Navajo dress borders are distinc-
tively their own, the motifs probably taken from Navajo coiled baskets (fig. 60). There are simple crosses,
terraced squares, and zigzag lines. The stress is on
horizontal rather than diagonal lines, and designs are

static rather than dynamic like those of the Pueblos.
Borders are woven in tapestry weave rather than
worked in embroidery. Embroidery apparently was
never adopted by Navajo women. The only similarity between the designs of the two groups is the use
of negative patterning, although in the case of the
Navajo the small dark figures set into the red border
bands are actually worked in indigo blue. The red
yarns are raveled from lac- or cochineal-dyed commercial cloth. Such yarns are much more prominent
in nineteenth-century Navajo weaving than in Pueblo work. The latter people used raveled red mainly
as embroidery yarns.

A second significant development around 1800
was the modification of the striped shoulder blanket
into what has become known as the chief blanket.
Dark (natural brown or black wool) horizontal stripes
were organized into a solid broad band at the blanket's center and bands half-again as wide along top
and bottom borders. Between the center and border
bands are somewhat narrower alternating black and
white stripes. As time went on designs were worked
into the center and border bands. These evolved in
complexity through what are known as Phase I, II,
III, and IV patterns.

Phase I designs were woven between 1800 and
1850. Narrow indigo blue stripes were sometimes
incorporated into the broad center and edge bands,
and in some instances the indigo stripes were edged
with narrow lines of raveled red. In Phase II (early
1800s to 1870) patterns, small red rectangles or bars
were woven into the indigo stripes, creating twelve
spots of color in the broad center and border bands
(fig. 72). Phase III (1860 to 1880) patterns are characterized by the insertion of nine figures, three in
the broad center band and three each in the border
bands (fig. 74). These commonly consist of a diamond at the center of the broad band, half-diamonds
at the edges of that band and the centers of top and
bottom borders, and quarter-diamonds at each corner of the blanket. Phase IV (1870 to 1875) simply
refers to the increasingly complex and varied nature
of the figures inserted in or placed over the horizontal stripes of the blanket. Chief blankets were a major

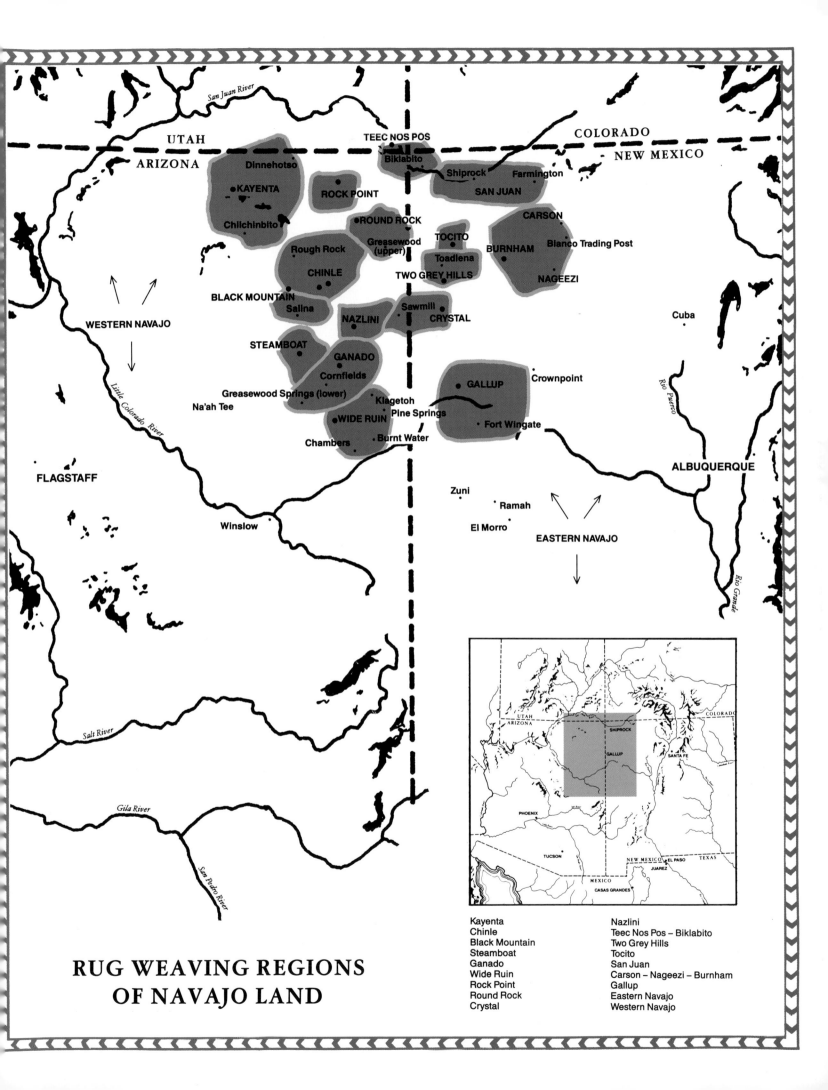

RUG WEAVING REGIONS
OF NAVAJO LAND

Kayenta
Chinle
Black Mountain
Steamboat
Ganado
Wide Ruin
Rock Point
Round Rock
Crystal

Nazlini
Teec Nos Pos – Biklabito
Two Grey Hills
Tocito
San Juan
Carson – Nageezi – Burnham
Gallup
Eastern Navajo
Western Navajo

Navajo Trade Fair at Bluff, Utah, 1902. At center, a pictorial rug
displays stylized cornstalk deities. Photograph by Charles Goodman.
Photo Archives, Museum of New Mexico.

article of trade with Ute and Plains Indians in the nineteenth century. They had the reputation of being so closely woven as to be waterproof.

The same simple terraced figures woven into women's dress borders were transferred to tapestry weave serapes after 1800 (fig. 49). They were used in increasingly complicated combinations through the 1850s. Technically superior both in spinning and weaving, serapes are outstanding examples of Navajo women's skills and were in great demand among Indians, Spaniards, and Anglo-Americans alike.

Serapes were usually woven of natural white and indigo-dyed handspun wool combined with lac- and cochineal-dyed raveled red. Occasionally a vegetal yellow handspun yarn appears and sometimes green, probably produced by combining indigo and yellow dyes. Commercial cloth in colors other than red was sometimes raveled, but red was definitely the preferred color.

After 1860 new materials appear in the serapes. The first of these are three-ply commercial yarns, some dyed with natural and some with chemical dyes. Four-ply aniline-dyed yarns appear after 1870, as do yarns raveled from American flannel. Fibers from commercial cloth which did not ravel well into usable yarns were also sometimes carded and spun with white wool to make a pinkish single-ply handspun yarn.

Mexican influence is evident in Navajo serapes before 1860. A very few were woven like a Mexican poncho with a slit at the center for the head. Design ideas taken from Mexican Saltillo blankets had affected Spanish weavers in the Rio Grande Valley early in the nineteenth century and from them passed to the Navajos (fig. 70). These ideas include the presence of a large central serrate diamond set on a background of vertical rows of small figures. By 1880 Saltillo characteristics begin to dominate Navajo blanket design.

Although they would undoubtedly have appeared

in Navajo weaving sooner or later, it is probable that the forcible incarceration of Navajos at Bosque Redondo in central New Mexico between 1863 and 1868 hastened the acquisition of commercial materials. Lacking sheep, they turned to using yarns and cloth issued by the U.S. Army. It may be that blankets with Saltillo patterns from Rio Grande looms were also given them at Bosque Redondo.

LATE HISTORIC PERIOD, 1880 TO 1960

With the coming of the railroad in 1880 Anglo-American influence, which had been strong since the 1860s, dominated Navajo weaving. Not only were commercial yarns available, but also packaged aniline dyes in a range of colors unknown to weavers in the earlier years of the nineteenth century. Some Navajo women wove into their blankets the novel things they saw around them—trains, letters from flour sacks and coffee cans, cattle brands, and other puzzling items (fig. 82).

Rail transport brought tourists to the Southwest and opened the markets of the eastern United States to Indian crafts. Hundreds of blankets were woven to meet the escalating demand. By the 1880s women did little weaving for their own use, clothing themselves and their families in factory-made materials and Pendleton blankets.

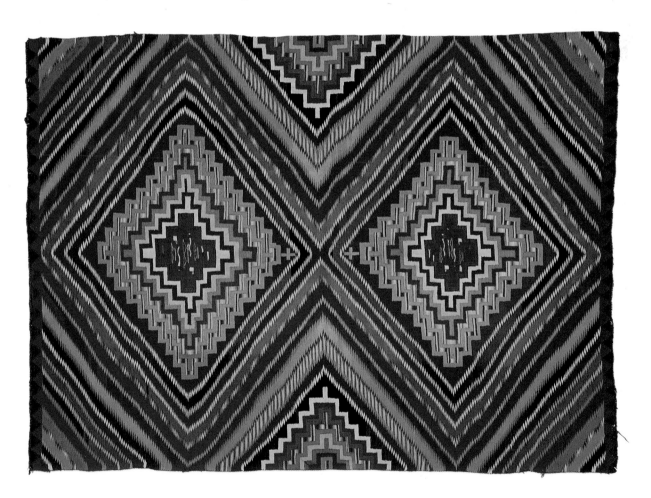

Germantown Blanket, 1880. Typical Germantown pieces of the period, made of commercial yarns, are characterized by riotous colors and sharply pointed serrate triangles.

The years from 1880 to 1900 saw experimentation with color, design, and even technique. Although the terraced patterns and horizontal stripes of earlier times did not disappear altogether, new dynamic compositions were devised, featuring sharp pointed triangles often organized into zigzag lines placed vertically on the blanket. Many weavings showed a riot of colors, imaginatively combined. Sometimes in order to use as many different hues as possible the weaver outlined each triangle motif with a contrasting color.

Two novelty weaves, seldom seen today, enjoyed limited popularity among weavers of the late 1880s. The first, two-faced weave, may have been learned from Anglo-Americans or Hispanics, as it is well known to artisans working on a four-harness horizontal treadle loom. When done on the Navajo vertical loom, four heddles were used, two throwing long weft floats to the surface of the textile, and two throwing long weft floats to the back. Thus one pattern could be developed on the front, and an entirely different pattern, usually of simple stripes, on the reverse side.

The second novelty process is called wedge weave. Without a precedent in the Southwest, it may well have been a Navajo invention (fig. 73). It is a way of weaving a band of oblique stripes of color without recourse to the tedious process of tapestry weave. In wedge weave wefts which are to form the stripes are simply beaten into the warps at an angle. In the succeeding band of stripes the angle is reversed. Warps are pulled to slant in one direction in the first band, the opposite direction in the second, and the edges of the blanket are thus "scalloped."

Traders, in answer to the American collectors' needs, urged the weaving of rugs rather than blankets (fig. 166). By 1900 the transition from blanket to rug was complete and a number of other trader-induced changes had occurred in Navajo weaving (fig. 83). The wild color schemes and dazzling compositions of the 1880s were frowned upon, and rugs were woven instead in black, gray, white, and red. Traders discouraged the presence of commercial yarns in rugs and fostered the use of native wool, which had previously lost its value on the off-reservation market.

Hopi weaver, 1897. Photograph by F. Maude. Photo Archives, Museum of New Mexico.

Under Anglo-American influence several design systems totally new to Navajo textiles appeared toward the end of the nineteenth century. One was the presence of solid borders on all four edges of a rug. This didn't fit well with the old principle of weaving in horizontal or vertical stripe patterns, which were an integral part of the background and simply ran off the ends or sides of the textile. Borders enclose a space which invites figures rather than stripes, and many Navajo rugs of the early 1900s were patterned by disconnected motifs floating on a solid color background rather than being a part of it.

It was at this time that *yei* (Navajo holy people) figures began to appear on rugs (fig. 95). This development was regarded with horror by many Navajos. It was said that weavers who thus transgressed tribal tenets would go blind. However, the Anglo-American tourists' fascination with native symbolism has assured the survival of *yei* and other religious motifs in Navajo weaving.

Perhaps the most significant design influence was that of J. B. Moore, trader at Crystal, New Mexico from 1897 to 1911. Moore exposed weavers around his post to the Oriental rug patterns which were popular in the eastern United States in the early 1900s. The motifs and designs developed by weavers as a result of his influence have become a familiar part of the twentieth-century Navajo design repertoire.

In the last half of the nineteenth and the early decades of the twentieth centuries the U.S. government had introduced new breeds of sheep onto the Navajo Reservation with the aim of increasing the yield of meat and wool. In so doing, however, they polluted the native churro sheep. The churro, originally imported from Spain via Mexico, were hardy animals which had adjusted well to the rigorous conditions of the Navajo homeland. Their wool was long staple and virtually greaseless, which meant it was easy to card and spin by hand methods and took dye well. Wool of the new breeds tended to be kinky and greasy. It resisted hand carding and spinning and took dye poorly. By the 1920s the quality of Navajo rugs had deteriorated markedly.

Seeking to reverse this unsatisfactory state of affairs, the U.S. government established the Southwestern Range and Sheep Breeding Laboratory in the 1930s to develop a breed of sheep with good, spinnable wool. Prior to this time private individuals interested in Navajo weaving had sought to improve dye quality, ultimately initiating experiments with vegetal dyes.

By the 1930s a number of distinctive styles of weaving were established, each named for the trading post or region in which it originated. Today these are standard types, although no longer woven only in one area.

CONTEMPORARY, 1960 TO PRESENT

Navajo weaving has maintained its importance as a vital native art to the present day. Virtually all the nineteenth- and twentieth-century styles of blan-

kets and rugs are still woven and new styles continue to appear (fig. 181). A recent trend is the weaving in very fine yarns of technically superb pieces intended as wall hangings (fig. 180).

Pueblo weaving, meanwhile, has declined almost to the vanishing point. A few Hopi men still produce traditional articles of clothing, and some Rio Grande Pueblo women weave belts and sashes and embroider handsome dance mantas. Like the embroidered mantas, most traditional Pueblo clothing is made nowadays of commercial fabrics. A comparison of modern dance costume with that of prehistoric figures depicted in kiva murals makes it clear, however, that while materials have changed, Pueblo costume, seen in the context of the dance, remains the same as in pre-Conquest times.

Navajo weaver, ca. 1926. Photo Archives, Museum of New Mexico.

Two Thousand Years of
Southwest Indian Arts and Culture

Plates

Photographs by Douglas Kahn

Fig. 1. Anasazi Necklaces, ca. 1050.
Black-and-white stone disc beads with olivella shells at
each end, from the Great Kiva at Chetro Ketl, Chaco
Canyon, New Mexico. The number of beads per
necklace ranges from 1,538 to 2,265. The lengths
vary from 7 feet to 16 feet, 1 inch.

THE PREHISTORIC PERIOD, 1000 B.C. TO A.D. 1540

Most of the prehistoric objects presented here were made during the first and second millennia A.D. It was a time of gradual but profound change for prehistoric southwesterners. As people settled down to permanent farming communities their population began to grow. Technology changed to support the increasing demands of a rapidly growing population. Prehistoric manufactures were primarily of stone, bone, shell, cotton fiber, ceramic, and materials derived from native plants and animals. Shells were imported from the coasts of California and Mexico. Cotton was grown locally and the fibers were spun and woven into cloth. Woven baskets had been the primary containers for centuries until around A.D. 500 when pottery was introduced from Mexico. Pottery containers quickly replaced baskets for food storage and preparation. (Broken pottery sherds are the most common archaeological artifact.) The forms of native craft objects closely followed their functions, and apparently nearly everyone was a craftsman. Although most of the manufactures probably were for domestic use, there also was a burgeoning trade in craft objects.

FIG. 2. BASKETMAKER II TRAY, 0–400.
This flat piece, found in a cave in Utah, is coiled with
a single rod and a splint or fiber bundle.

FIG 3. BASKETMAKER III COILED BASKET, 500–700.
A small coiled basket of typical Basketmaker style,
this piece is coiled with two rods and a bundle and
finished at the top with a very flat herringbone rim.
Found in south central New Mexico.

FIG. 4. BASKETMAKER TWILLED RING BASKET, 0–700.

FIG. 5. BASKETMAKER III YUCCA RING BASKET, 500–700.
These baskets were first made during this period. This
one is twill plaited with yucca. Bat Woman House,
Water Lily Canyon, Arizona.

FIG. 6. ALMA PLAIN OLLA, 450–500.
This water jar, found in west-central New Mexico,
was produced by the Mogollon Culture.

FIG. 7. ROSA SMOOTHED JAR, A.D. 600–700.
This jar dates from the Basketmaker III period from
northwestern New Mexico.

FIG. 8. LINO GRAY PITCHER, 500–700.
This Anasazi example was excavated at Allantown
Ruin in east-central Arizona.

FIG. 9. KANA-A GRAY PITCHER, 750–850.
Another Anasazi piece from the Allantown Ruin.

FIG. 10. KIATUTHLANNA BLACK-ON-WHITE BOWL, 750–850.
Anasazi, from Allantown Ruin.

FIG. 11. MANGAS BLACK-ON-WHITE BOWL, 750–950.
A Mimbres example, found near Silver City,
New Mexico.

FIG. 12. THREE CIRCLE NECK CORRUGATED JAR, 900–1000.
From a cave near Silver City, New Mexico.

FIG. 13. BASKETMAKER YUCCA SANDAL WITH PAINTED SOLE, 500–700.
The inner surface of sandals with knotted soles bears a
tapestry-weave design totally unrelated to that made by the knots.

Fig. 14. Red Mesa Black-on-white Beaker, 950–1050.

FIG. 15. HOHOKAM SHELL FROG, 900–1100.
Carved from one half of a bivalve shell. From Martinez
Hill site, Arizona.

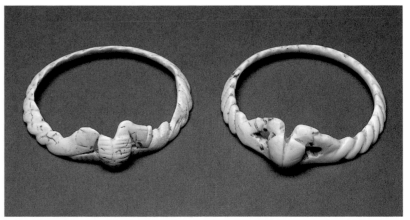

FIG. 16. PAIR OF MIMBRES SHELL BRACELETS, 1000–1150.
Glycymeris gigantus shells are carved to create a twisted
effect, and each has a zoomorphic effigy at the umbo.
From Cameron Creek ruin, New Mexico.

FIG. 17. WINGATE BLACK-ON-RED SEED JAR, 1050–1150.

Fig. 18. Gallup Black-on-white Seed Jar, 950–1100.

Fig. 19. Chaco Corrugated Jar, 1000–1150.

FIG. 20. MIMBRES BLACK-ON-WHITE BOWL, 1000–1150.

FIG. 21. MIMBRES BLACK-ON-WHITE BOWL, 1000–1150.
The pictorial representation may be of an emergence myth.

FIG. 22. MIMBRES BLACK-ON-WHITE BOWL, 1000–1150.
The bowl depicts game players or arrow makers.

113

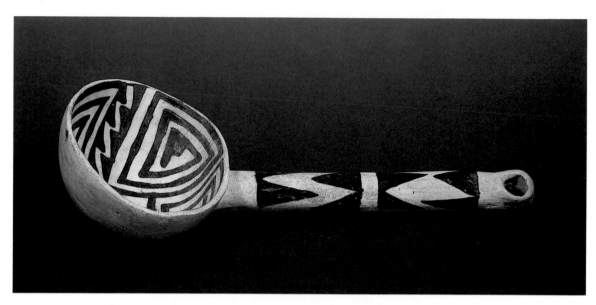

FIG. 23. CHACO MCELMO BLACK-ON-WHITE DIPPER, 1075–1200.
This dipper has a hollow handle containing a pebble
rattle of clay or stone. It is from McKinley County,
New Mexico.

FIG. 24. TULAROSA BLACK-ON-WHITE EFFIGY, 1150–1250.

FIG. 25. ST. JOHNS POLYCHROME BOWL, 1200–1275.

FIG. 26. MIMBRES BLACK-ON-WHITE BOWL, 1000–1150.

FIG. 27. SOCORRO BLACK-ON-WHITE BOWL, 1100–1250.

FIG. 28. MIMBRES BLACK-ON-WHITE CANTEEN, 1000–1150.

116

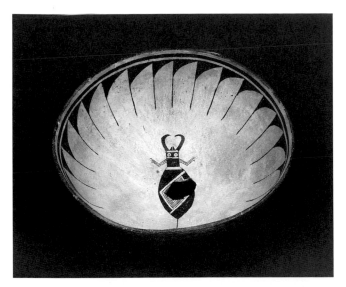

FIG. 29. MIMBRES BLACK-ON-WHITE BOWL, 1000–1150.

FIG. 30. MIMBRES BLACK-ON-WHITE BOWL, 1000–1150.

FIG. 31. BANDELIER BLACK-ON-CREAM BOWL, CA. 1450–1550.

117

FIG. 32. ANASAZI WATER JAR, 1000–1300.
This large, pear-shaped twined jar was heavily pitched
with piñon gum after being coated with red clay.
From a cave in the Lukachukai Mountains,
New Mexico.

FIG. 33. ANASAZI TURKEY FEATHER BLANKET, 1250–1300.
Cordage for this Anasazi (Pueblo III) blanket from Jemez Cave was
made by wrapping feathers tightly around yucca-fiber twine. This
piece served as the outer wrapping of an infant burial.

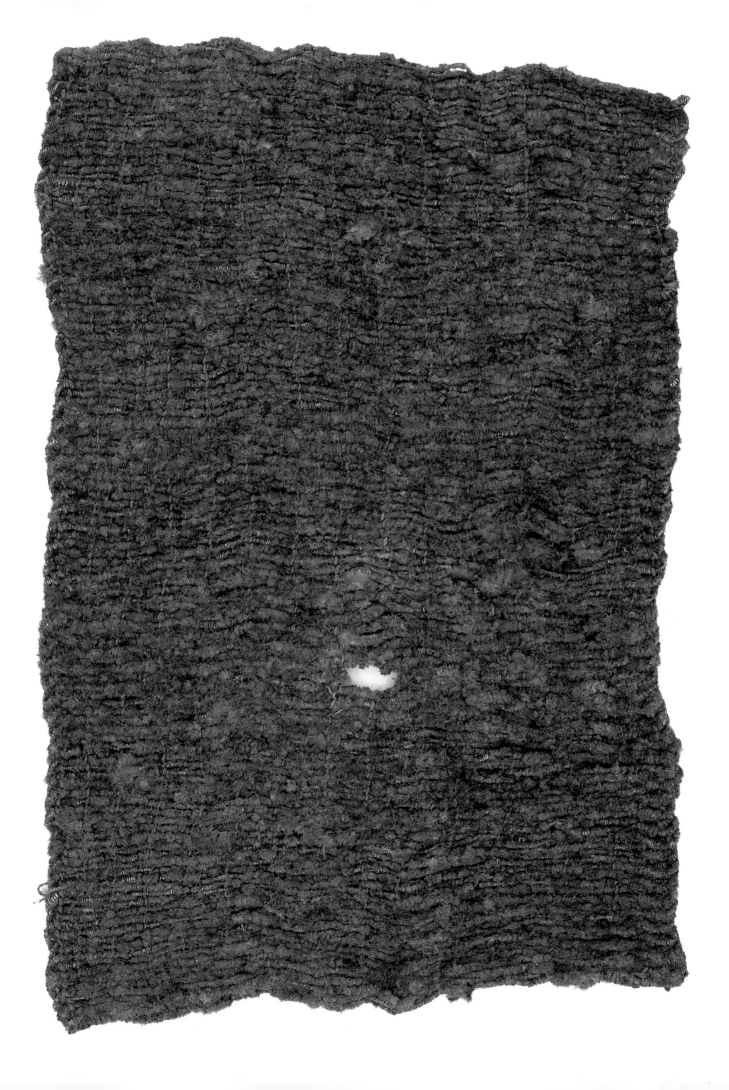

FIG. 34. ANASAZI BONE COLLAR, 1400–1600.
This piece from the Pecos Ruin, New Mexico, consists
of a mammal rib bone bent to form a semicircular
collar, the ends perforated for tying.

FIG. 35. ANASAZI MICA DRESS ORNAMENT, 1600s.
This piece is perforated around the edges for
attachment to a garment. It is a prehistoric style that
continued to be popular into historic times.

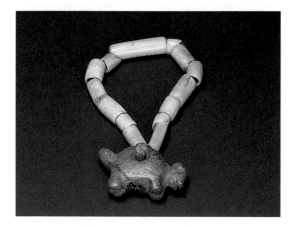

FIG. 36. CHIHUAHUAN NECKLACE AND PENDANT, 1200–1450.
The stone mountain sheep pendant, from near Casas
Grandes, Mexico, is attached to a strand of shells from
Casas Grandes ruin.

Fig. 37. Klageto Black-on-white Stirrup Canteen, 1200–1300.

FIG. 38. LOOPED BAG, ANIMAS PHASE, 1200–1425. Made from two-ply apocynum fiber cordage, one ply red and the other natural tan, this Mogollon bag from U-Bar Cave contained a pipe when found. The bag was made by a simple looping technique. Two prehistoric mends may be seen near its base.

FIG. 39. PREHISTORIC BASKET, ANIMAS PHASE, 1200–1425. The small size, wedge shape, the two-rod-and-bundle construction are characteristic of ceremonial baskets of the Basketmaker III period. The basket contained the pelts of two ring-tailed cats and the large net of human hair (fig. 41) when found at U-Bar Cave, New Mexico.

FIG. 40. TLALOC EFFIGY, 1200–1425.
Found in U-Bar Cave in 1960, this effigy figure is
made of split yucca or sotol stalk splints sewn with
fibers. The large eyes indicate that this figure
represents Tlaloc, the Mesoamerican Rain God. It
suggests a Southwestern ceremonial use of caves in the
quest for rain similar to that found in Mesoamerica.

FIG. 41. HUMAN HAIR HUNTING NET, ANIMAS PHASE, 1200–1425.
There are about 1.54 miles of hair cordage in this
Mogollon net from U-Bar Cave, requiring about
sixty-nine heads of hair. Nets of this kind were
stretched out in a semicircle or open V. Rabbits driven
against the net were clubbed to death.

THE EARLY HISTORIC PERIOD,
1598 TO 1880

The Early Historic Period witnessed important changes in Southwest Indian material culture as European manufactured goods replaced many traditional technologies and craft arts. By the late 1800s basket-making, the oldest of all southwestern crafts, had declined or disappeared throughout most of the South-west. Pottery making suffered a similar decline following the introduction of machine-made ceramic and metal containers. The weaving of textiles for cloth-ing and blankets virtually disappeared among the Pueblos in the 1800s. There was, however, a vigor-ous development of the weaving arts among the Nav-ajo, who had adopted the pueblo-style upright loom in the early 1700s and substituted domestic wool for native cotton. Perhaps the only traditional craft that was not transformed by Euro-American contact was the production of traditional ornamentation. In the ear-ly 1800s metal working was added to the list of tra-ditional crafts, but Indian craftsmen continued to work the more traditional materials of shell, stone, bone, and horn.

FIG. 42. PITCH COVERED NAVAJO WATER JAR, CA. 1700.
This jar was found in a cave in the Jemez Mountains,
and because of its shape is thought to be Navajo.

FIG. 43. EARLY PUEBLO BASKET, 1700–1850.
The final coils of this two-rod-and-bundle basket,
which probably formed a slightly flaring neck, have
been broken off. A design of rectangular meanders can
be seen around its sides. Probably used to hold beads,
fetishes, or medicines.

FIG. 44. HAWIKUH (GLAZE) POLYCHROME, CA. 1680.
Hawikuh, an ancient Zuni village, is the name given
to this type of pottery done both at Zuni and Acoma.
This jar, collected at Acoma, is representative of one
of the finest statements made by Pueblo potters and
signifies the end of the glazeware tradition at
Acoma and Zuni.

FIG. 45. AKO POLYCHROME, CA. 1770.
A "mushroom" shape with a sculpted rim
distinguishes this Acoma Pueblo jar. The design,
especially the "rainbird," is probably inspired by
Zuni motifs.

FIG. 46. POWHOGE POLYCHROME, SAN ILDEFONSO VARIETY, 1770–1790.
This is an early example of the type, with a low rounded
bottom, tall sloping shoulder, and feathers in the design.
The banded geometric design was done with vegetal paint
on hard stone-stroked white slip.

FIG. 47. TEWA POLYCHROME BOWL, 17TH CENTURY.
This vessel was found on the floor of an apparent
westward expansion of the Palace of the Governors
in Santa Fe.

FIG. 48. ZIA (TRIOS) POLYCHROME STORAGE JAR, CA. 1800.
The height of this jar, its convex base, panelled body
design, and short neck with a separate design suggest
an early date for this piece.

FIG. 49. NAVAJO LATE CLASSIC SERAPE, 1860–1866.
Woven during the time the Navajos were incarcerated
at Bosque Redondo.

128

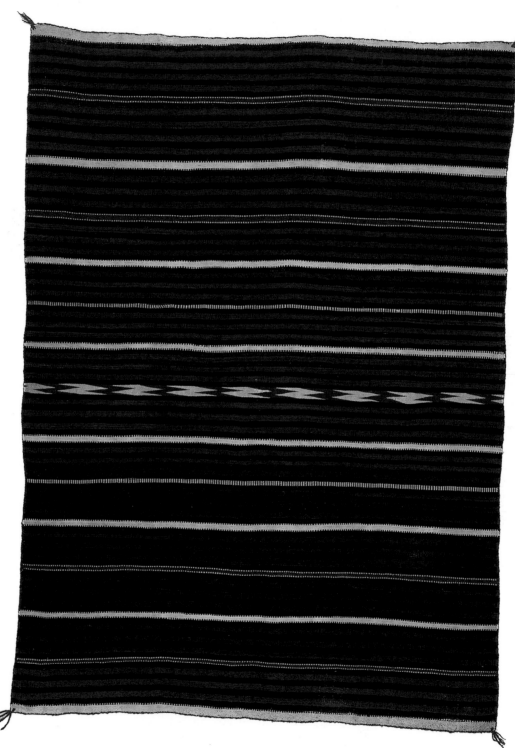

FIG. 50. NAVAJO "MOQUI"-STYLE BLANKET, 1850S.
The pattern of narrow stripes in indigo blue, natural
brown, and white was called "Moqui-pattern" by
19th-century traders who mistakenly assumed such
blankets were woven by the Pueblos, principally
the Hopi or "Moqui."

FIG. 51. ZIA POLYCHROME, CA. 1870.
This pot's rounded form with short neck suggests an
early date, but the developed bird motifs, which may
derive from imported cloth designs, indicate a more
recent date of manufacture.

FIG. 52. ACOMA POLYCHROME, 1875–1880.
The thinner construction, more graceful transitions
between body sections, and tall neck of this vessel are
typical of post-Acomita Polychrome pieces. The jar
features bird and floral motifs and an undulating
"rainbow band" possibly inspired by New Mexico
colcha embroidery, a Spanish Colonial
textile technique.

131

FIG. 53. NAVAJO BASKET, MID–19TH CENTURY.
The distinctive features of these baskets are their
two-rod-and-bundle coiling, flat herringbone rim, and
designs of vegetal-dyed sumac splints.

FIG. 54. NAVAJO BASKET, MID–19TH CENTURY.
Navajos did not depend on Paiutes for their supply of
baskets until after 1890. They continued to make a
few for their own use.

FIG. 55. EARLY HISTORIC HOPI BASKET, MID–1800S.
This type of plaited wicker basket is still typical of
Hopi villages on Third Mesa today. It was made with
warps of sumac and wefts of rabbit brush, and the rim
is bound with yucca splints.

FIG. 56. NAVAJO COOKING POT, PLAINWARE, 1850–1900.
This is a typical cooking pot with rounded bottom to
place in the fire for even heating. The coil decoration
around the neck may also aid in the handling of the
hot pot during use.

FIG. 57. ACOMA EMBROIDERED COTTON MANTA, CA. 1850.
Figures like the two birds on this manta generally distinguish pieces from
Acoma Pueblo. Negative patterning, in which small lines of white ground
cloth between embroidered areas actually form the design, is an ancient
Pueblo technique, found on contemporary Pueblo embroidery as well.

FIG. 58. ZUNI EMBROIDERED WOOL MANTA, CA. 1870.
A basic traditional article of Pueblo dress is the
manta, a rectangular blanket woven wider than long,
used by men and women as a shoulder robe and by
women folded about the body as a dress.

FIG. 59. EARLY HISTORIC PUEBLO BURDEN BASKET, 1850–1880.
This Pueblo basket is woven with a combination of
twilled and plain twine. It has a single-rod rim bound
to the warps which are brought up to below the rim,
then bent and plaited over and under two sets of
adjacent warps.

FIG. 60. WOVEN WOOL DRESS, CA. 1850.
This dress contains black and indigo handspun wool yarns, raveled
red, and narrow green lines of weft at the inner edges of the border
that are vegetal-dyed handspun wool. Designs on the borders of
Navajo dresses were apparently taken from their coiled baskets.

134

FIG. 61. ZUNI POLYCHROME, CA. 1870.
The severe underbody, bulbous but squared-off body,
and flexure at the neck seen here are typical of Zuni
jars. The painting on this piece is exceptional, in
black and red slip with typical separate neck band and
panelled body design featuring "rainbird" motifs.

FIG. 63. NAVAJO BRACELET, 1860S.
This heavy brass bracelet decorated with a simple filed design is an excellent example of the earliest type of Navajo metal work. It is probably fashioned from a ramrod.

FIG. 64. NAVAJO BRACELET, 1880S.
Each end of this silver wire bangle has been flattened and filed to form "hands."

FIG. 65. NAVAJO BRACELET, 1870S.
This very early cast-silver bracelet is set with two rough native garnets. It is one of the earliest known examples of stones set in silver.

FIG. 66. NAVAJO BRACELET, 1870S.
Decorated only with dies and cold chisel, this silver band bracelet is in a general style that was common before 1900.

FIG. 62. CONCHA BELT, 1860–1880.
This belt belonged to Manuelito, a famous chief of the Navajos (d. 1893). The ten Plains-style conchas are of German silver, an alloy of copper, zinc, and nickel.

FIG. 67. NAVAJO EARRINGS, 1890S.
Flat silver loops with simple stamped designs on one surface. 1⅞" diameter.

FIG. 68. EARLY HISTORIC HOPI YUCCA-RING BASKET, 1880s–1890s.
This basket, plain plaited with narrow splints, is a
type rarely made in recent times. Collected
about 1890.

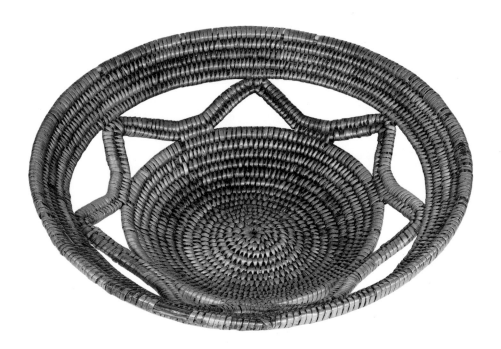

FIG. 69. JICARILLA APACHE BASKET, LATE 19TH CENTURY.
This open-work basket shows three-rod-bunch
construction. Its aniline dyes have faded into soft
colors. Such open work was rare, and used to make
sewing baskets for tourists.

Fig. 70. Navajo Classic Period Poncho, 1840–1860.
This blanket, woven as a poncho with a head slit at the center, is a
Mexican form, but a few Navajo-woven examples survive from the
Classic period. All yarns are handspun but the red, which is raveled
from lac-dyed commercial cloth.

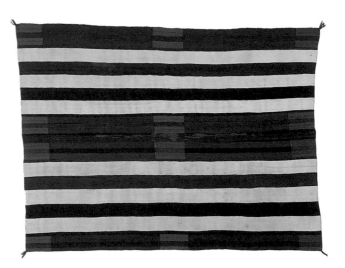

FIG. 71. WOVEN MANTA, CA. 1870–1880.
This piece of diagonal twill weave with diamond twill
borders was worn about the shoulders. The pattern of
terraced triangles can be compared with that in Navajo
dress border designs. This manta was collected
in Taos in 1892.

FIG. 72. NAVAJO CHIEF BLANKET, PHASE II, 1860–1865.
In the 19th century, Phase II chief blankets such as
this were woven with small bars or rectangles of red at
the ends and centers of the broad center and edge
bands, thus creating a twelve-spot pattern.

FIG. 73. NAVAJO WOMAN'S SHOULDER BLANKET, LATE 1880S.
The pattern of black and gray zigzag lines in this
blanket was produced by wedge weave, in which wefts
are battened diagonally, rather than horizontally,
into the warps.

FIG. 74. NAVAJO CHIEF BLANKET, PHASE III, 1870–1880.
Between about 1860 and 1880 chief blanket patterns
were characterized by nine blocks of color, often a
terraced diamond in the center band, and quarter
diamonds at the four blanket corners.

reaching the Southwest in the 1880s.

FIG. 76. EARLY HISTORIC HOPI SECOND MESA BASKET, CA. 1885.
This large basket was coiled with bundles of galleta
grass, sewn with strips of yucca, and decorated in a
typical Hopi design. Narrow coils were also
made at this time. The unfinished
ending is thought to signify that the maker was an
unmarried woman who had not yet had children.

Fig. 77. Laguna Polychrome, ca. 1880.
Rock additions in the tempering material of this pot
and slightly heavy construction suggest a Laguna
origin. The bold black geometric design is common at
both Acoma and Laguna during this period.

FIG. 78. SANTA ANA POLYCHROME, CA. 1870–1880.
This rare example of Santa Ana pottery features a
typical form with a design layout of arcs around the
neck and bold red motifs with unbordered open areas
on the body.

FIG. 79. JICARILLA APACHE WATER BOTTLE, CA. 1880.
The Jicarilla were long considered among the most
adventurous basket makers.

FIG. 80. TESUQUE POLYCHROME BOWL, CA. 1880.
This bowl is a classic example of Tesuque pottery with
a durable rippled stone-stroked slip. The
"free-floating" deep black vegetal designs are typical
of this type of pottery.

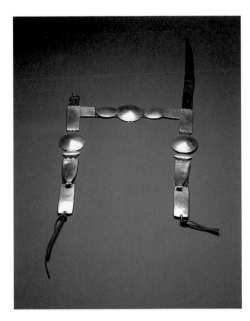

FIG. 81. NAVAJO BRIDLE, 1870s.
This silver mounted bridle shows a very early form of
decoration called "rocker" engraving. It has tapered
tabs extending down from the cheek straps, ending in
hand-shaped ornaments. The bridle is reliably
attributed to Atsidi Chon, a famed Navajo silversmith
who has been credited with making the first Navajo
silver headstall and first silver belt.

FIG. 82. NAVAJO EARLY PICTORIAL BLANKET, CA. 1880.
With the coming of the railroad, new materials and
pictorial design motifs, including trains themselves,
appeared in Navajo weaving. This blanket was
purchased at an auction in Boston in the early 1880s.

FIG. 83. GERMANTOWN BLANKET, POST 1880.
Woven in the 1880s, all materials in this blanket
are commercial.

THE LATE HISTORIC PERIOD,
1880 TO 1960

The coming of the railroad in the 1880s had a profound impact on native arts and crafts in the Southwest. The flood of Anglo settlers and tourists into the Southwest after 1880 resulted in a growing demand for traditional Indian arts and a revival of many traditional crafts. Old forms were modified to meet the needs and changing tastes of the tourist market, so that form no longer followed function. Encouraged by Anglo traders to produce a more marketable textile for the tourist market, Navajo weavers shifted from blanket to rug manufacture in the late nineteenth century. Basketmaking was revived at the turn of the century, with the manufacture of many non-utilitarian forms to satisfy the requirements of tourists. Perhaps the greatest craft revival at this time was in pottery making. New sizes and forms of pottery vessels appeared after the 1880s, many old pottery styles were resurrected for the commercial market, and new commercial demands spurred technical innovation.

FIG. 84. SAN JUAN BLACKWARE STORAGE JAR, 1890–1900.
This large, bulbous form is slipped on the upper half and
floated on the lower half. In the reducing fire (caused by
smothering the fire with powdered horse manure) carbon
penetrates the surface.

FIG. 85. SANTO DOMINGO POLYCHROME DOUGH BOWL, CA. 1890.
This is Santo Domingo pottery at its best; a high
floated underbody, wide red underbody band, and
strong simple geometric painting.

FIG. 86. HOPI BURDEN BASKET, CA. 1880–1910.
This traditional basket is a type frequently referred to
as a "peach basket." It is coarsely plaited with sumac
and reinforced with two U-shaped juniper rods. The
simple design was made by scraping the bark
from the wefts.

146

FIG. 87. ZIA POLYCHROME STORAGE JAR, CA. 1910.
This jar is a magnificent example of realistic painting
with geometric motifs. The deer motif may have been
inspired by colcha embroidery, a textile technique in
Spanish Colonial New Mexico.

FIG. 88. MESCALERO APACHE BOWL, 1895.
This shallow bowl, collected in 1899, features
animal-form designs in natural yellow yucca and deep
red yucca root.

FIG. 89. APACHE MICACEOUS JAR, 1880–1900.
This jar, possibly inspired by the wares of Taos and
Picuris, is modelled closely after Apache basketry
ollas, which are sealed with pitch and used as
water containers.

FIG. 90. HOPI PLAINWARE CANTEEN, CA. 1900.
This type of canteen has been made for centuries and
exact dating is difficult, but the high domed form
with spout and two handles is typical at Hopi. Such
canteens were used for water storage and as receptacles
for snakes during the Snake Dance.

FIG. 91. NAVAJO WATER BOTTLE, 1890–1915.
Made with three-rod coils and entirely covered inside
and out with piñon pitch, this basket is of a type
which was made and used by the Navajos and the
Southern Paiutes for many years.

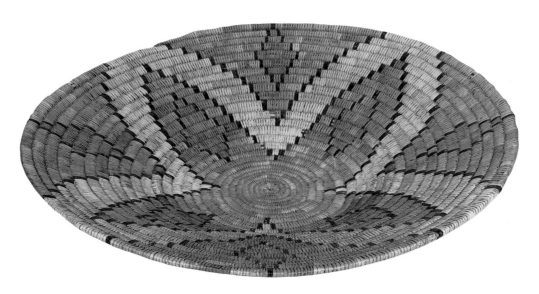

FIG. 92. MESCALERO APACHE TRAY, CA. 1900.
This classic Mescalero tray has a four-petaled figure
outlined in a red yucca root. These baskets were used
by the Mescaleros on ceremonial occasions.

149

FIG. 93. SANTA CLARA BLACKWARE JAR, CA. 1900.
This is a classic example of the exaggerated form that
has become a Santa Clara tradition. The jar, according
to potter Margaret Tafoya, was made by her mother
Serafina Tafoya. The impressed bear-paw motifs are
used on water jars because "the bear always knows
where the water is."

FIG. 94. SAN ILDEFONSO BLACK-ON-BLACK JAR, CA. 1918–1919.
This is one of Maria Martinez's first Black-on-black
jars, painted by her husband Julian. It depicts the
Awanyu (Plumed Water Serpent) that has become a
trademark of Martinez pottery and San Ildefonso
pottery design in general.

FIG. 95. NAVAJO EARLY YEI PATTERN RUG, CA. 1900.
Over the objections of many tribal members, a few
Navajo women began to weave Yei, or Holy People,
figures into their textiles around 1900. This is an early
example of the type.

FIG. 96. MESCALERO APACHE COILED "BOX," CA. 1915.
These unusual "boxes" have coils made with thin, flat
slats of wood. They are stitched with the usual
yucca splints.

FIG. 97. NAVAJO BRACELET, 1900–1920s.
This grooved silver band was stamped, then bent, to shape. The flat turquoise is set in a hand-cut toothed bezel.

FIG. 98. NAVAJO BRACELET, 1930s.
This tourist example is made of white metal with stamped grooves. It is decorated with stamped motifs such as the prominent, non-traditional arrows.

FIG. 99. NAVAJO SILVER COMB, 1910–1920.
This comb is characterized by stamped and repoussé leaf designs and four turquoise sets.

FIG. 100. WHITE BRAIDED SASH, POST 1900.
White braided sashes with heavy fringes, such as this one, often called rain sashes, circle the waist. Such sashes were traditionally supplied to Rio Grande Pueblos by Hopi weavers.

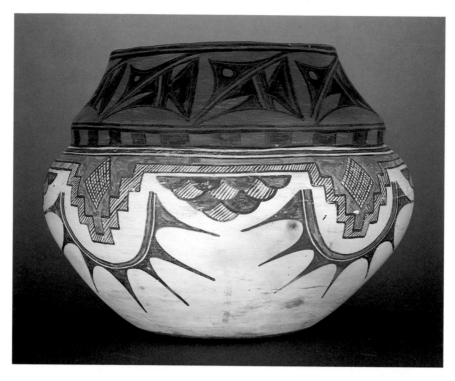

Fig. 101. San Ildefonso Polychrome (in two slips) Jar, ca. 1918.
This unusual jar by Maria and Julian Martinez combines the newly
introduced Cochiti rag-wiped slip (rather than the more difficult San
Ildefonso stone-stroked slip) and the San Ildefonso red slip. It is
signed Poh-ve-ha, or Pond Lily (Maria's Indian name).

Fig. 102. San Ildefonso Wicker Basket, ca. 1917.
This unusually large basket of plaited willow branches
was very possibly made by famous basketmaker
Pasqual Martinez. It is the enduring type in the
Rio Grande pueblos.

FIG. 103. WHITE COTTON KILT, POST 1880.
A white cotton kilt with embroidered ends is a
standard item of wear for male dancers in
all the pueblos.

FIG. 104. SANTA CLARA POLISHED PLAINWARE TRAIN, 1900–1920.
According to potter Margaret Tafoya, this piece was made by her aunt Santana
Gutierrez. It is a realistic rendering of a train, with the engine and coal cart in
reduced Blackware and the caboose in oxydized Redware. The piece is typical of
commercial wares made strictly for the tourist trade.

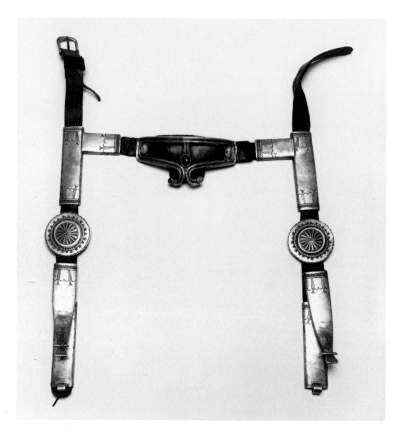

FIG. 105. NAVAJO HEADSTALL, 1900–1920s.
This silver mounted headstall is made of flat sheet
silver, decorated with die work. Silver ornaments are
hung from the cheek straps. There is a round stamped
concha on each side. The cast silver brow band has five
turquoise sets.

FIG. 106. NAVAJO KETOH, 1890–1900.
This wrist guard is made of wrought silver with a
simple tooled-and-stamped design; it is mounted on a
leather band.

FIG. 107. NAVAJO KETOH, 1900–1920s.
Wrought silver wrist guard with stamped
and repoussé decoration. A row of eight stamped
fluted silver buttons are on a strap at the side
of the mounting.

FIG. 108. NAVAJO CAST SILVER KETOH, 1900–1920s.
This exceptionally fine and delicate cast-silver
wrist guard, representing a peak in the art of casting
in stone molds, has one small turquoise set in a
hand-cut bezel.

FIG. 109. NAVAJO KETOH, 1900–1920s.
This cast silver wrist guard is set with a large
turquoise in a plain bezel. It is attached to a leather
band, the edges of which are outlined by incising.

FIG. 110. JICARILLA APACHE STRAW HAT, EARLY 20TH CENTURY.
This flat-top straw hat was made for the tourist trade.
It was too heavy and stiff to be worn.

FIG. 111. JICARILLA APACHE LAUNDRY HAMPER, 1885–1920.
Made to sell to local farm families, this typical laundry
hamper has a lid and handles on both sides for lifting.

FIG. 112. NECKLACE OF SHELL AND TURQUOISE, CA. 1900.
Studded with turquoise and long slivers of cut shell,
this necklace is a type that Navajos or Pueblos might
have worn during the 1800s.

159

FIG. 113. NAVAJO SILVER BRACELET, 1900–1920s.
This silver band has simple stamped grooves.

FIG. 114. HOPI SECOND MESA BASKET, CA. 1920.
This old basket has a central design of pronghorn
antelope heads. Made at Shungopovi.

FIG. 115. HOPI YUCCA RING BASKET, 1920.
The narrow splints and complex pattern of concentric
crosses identifies this as a Hopi rather than a Rio
Grande basket.

FIG. 116. WESTERN APACHE BOWL, 1900–1920.
The design of this piece consists of a central star figure
with an outline and a series of small human figures
holding hands, crosses, and quadruped animals.

Fig. 117. Western Apache Tray, 1900–1920.
The checkered triangles on this large tray are typical of
Apache design, as are the human and animal figures
enclosed in other triangles. The basket maker
misjudged the size of one triangle and had to shorten
one of the animals, probably before she discovered that
her space was limited.

FIG. 118. *FROM LEFT* : NAVAJO CONCHA BELT, 1920S.
Oval silver conchas have sharp scalloped edges; filed,
stamped, and punched. Closed centers are
diamond-shaped, each set with an oval turquoise
in a plain bezel. Each concha has a cut-to-fit
leather backing. Rectangular silver buckle, filed
and stamped, set with four oval turquoises, also
has a leather backing.

COCHITI SILVER AND TURQUOISE CONCHA BELT, 1951.
This concha belt by Stanley Suina features round
conchas of silver overlay, each with one central
turquoise set, and a butterfly-shaped overlaid buckle
with turquoise sets.

NAVAJO CONCHA BELT, 1920S.
Typical 20th-century style: the oval silver conchas
have scalloped edges decorated with stamped dots and
other die work; the closed centers display stamped and
repoussé fusiform designs; copper bars are soldered on
the reverse of each, for stringing. These conchas
alternate with silver "butterfly" plaques, stamped and
repoussé. The oval buckle is filed and stamped.

NAVAJO SILVER CONCHA BELT, 1880S.
This early style belt features round silver conchas
rather than the more common ovals. Conchas have
filed, scalloped edges; punched and stamped
decoration; and cut-out diamond centers. They have
cut-to-fit leather backings.

163

FIG. 119. NAVAJO BRACELET, 1900–1920s.
A bracelet consisting of three narrow, twisted silver
wires set with three oval, cabochon-cut turquoises in
plain bezels, separated by silver teardrops.

FIG. 120. NAVAJO SILVER AND TURQUOISE BRACELET, 1910–1920s.
This bracelet has carinated silver bars with twisted silver wire
between them, a stamped design, and cabochon-cut turquoise
separated by silver teardrops.

FIG. 121. NAVAJO BRACELET, 1920s.
This Zuni-style Navajo bracelet was made from two
silver wires. It is decorated with three clusters of
turquoise mounted on silver plaques, and with small
appliqué silver wire scallops.

FIG. 122. ZUNI SILVER AND TURQUOISE BRACELET, 1920s–1930s.
This cluster-style bracelet consists of five plain round
silver wires on which are mounted turquoises flanked
by stamped vertical bars, each of these set with five
round turquoises and a rectangular turquoise set in an
octagonal stamped-silver mounting.

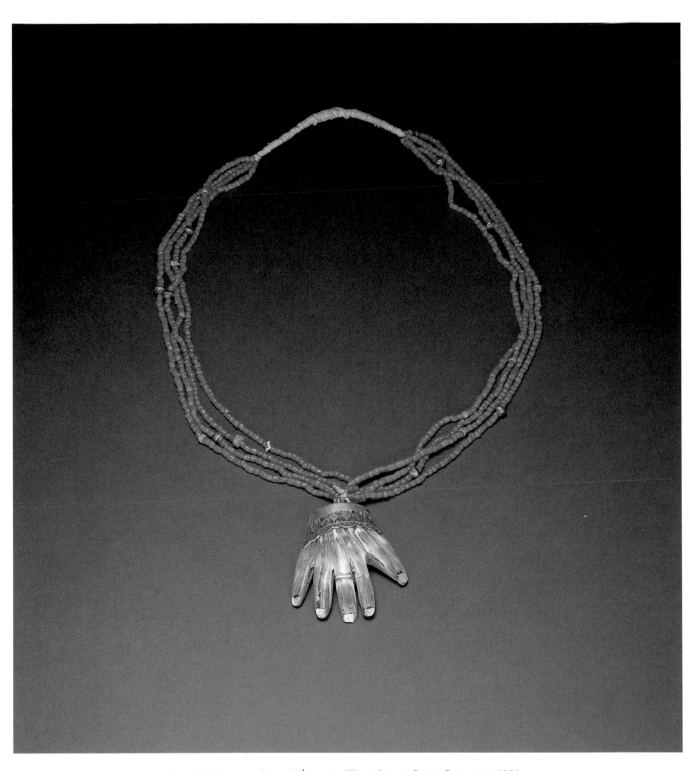

FIG. 123. PUEBLO CORAL NECKLACE WITH INLAID SHELL PENDANT, 1920S.
This handsome and very unusual necklace consists of four strands of
coral beads interspersed with silver and turquoise beads. A large
hand-shaped pendant of shell is set in silver decorated with stamped
designs. The hand has nacreous shell fingernails and an inlaid
turquoise ring.

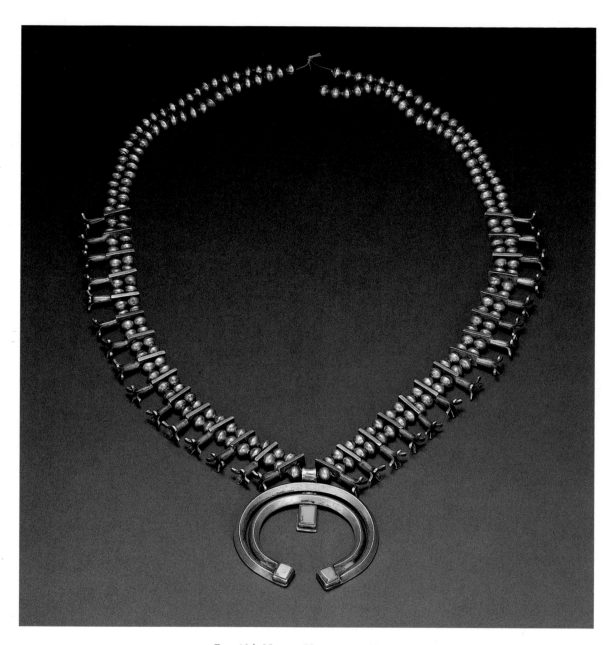

FIG. 124. NAVAJO NECKLACE, 1920s.
A style of squash blossom necklace popular during this period: two strands of very small silver beads interspersed with—and strung through soldered sheet-metal extensions of—silver squash blossoms. The *najahe* is made from two triangular pieces of silver wire bent to shape and soldered at each end. There are three turquoise sets: one at each end and one in the center soldered to a long thin strip of sheet metal that also acts as a jump ring.

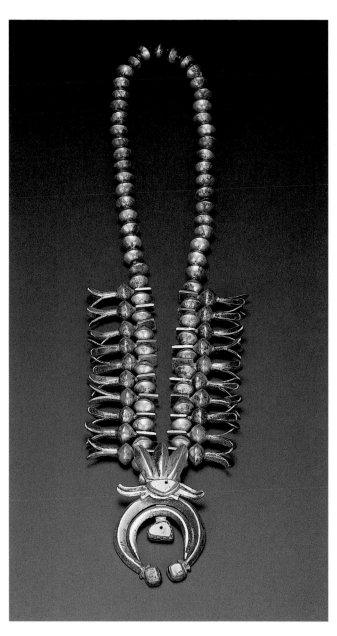

Fig. 126. Zuni-style Silver and Turquoise Earrings, 1920s–1930s.

Fig. 125. Navajo Necklace, 1920s.
Necklace of sharply shouldered silver beads. Silver
squash blossoms are cut from rolled sheet metal,
curled, and soldered to beads with sheet metal jump
rings. Cast silver double *najahe* has a stamped
half-butterfly at the top.

167

FIGS. 127, 128. HOPI THIRD MESA BASKET, 1920.
The figure on this plaited wicker tray depicts the
traditional hair style of unmarried women and wears
the Maiden's Shawl around her shoulders.

FIG. 129. HOPI SECOND MESA BASKET, 1925.
With its design of pronghorn antelopes and rain
terraces, this is a typical deep Hopi bowl.

FIG. 130. WESTERN APACHE BOWL, 1900–1925.

FIG. 131. JICARILLA APACHE LAUNDRY BASKET, CA. 1920.
This large, shallow basket has a distinctive Jicarilla
kind of handle on each side, ideal for carrying laundry.
The loop handles were made by pulling up a section of
the final coil and wrapping it separately.

FIG. 132. WESTERN APACHE OLLA, 1900–1925.
This is a good example of the lower, broader type of
olla, with a characteristic network design of negative
crosses in triangles. The dark color suggests that the
sewing material used in this basket may be mulberry.

FIG. 133. WESTERN APACHE OLLA, 1910–1925.
This large jar features typical Western Apache vertical
bands and design motifs including animal and human
figures, crosses, and birds.

FIG. 134. SASH, 1930.
Pueblo dance sash decorated with the typical brocade
design that is a stylized version of the Hopi Broad-face
Kachina mask.

FIG. 135. SICHOMOVI POLYCHROME (HOPI) SEED JAR, 1910–1915.
This is an outstanding example by the noted potter
Nampeyo. The black and white paint on red slip was
popular with Nampeyo in the period 1910 to 1915
but was done by other potters and continues to be
done today. The squat, oval form was popular at
Sikyatki (1325–1625) and inspired the revival efforts
of Nampeyo that made her an important force in
contemporary pottery.

172

FIG. 136. PUEBLO NECKLACE, 1920s–1930s.
This necklace consists of small shell disc beads
alternating with graduated turquoise discs. Its
pendant is a beautifully carved shell bird inlaid with
turquoise and jet.

FIG. 137. PUEBLO NECKLACE, 1920s–1930s.
An exceptionally fine necklace consisting of
two strands of shell disc beads strung through
fifty-eight turquoise mosaic-on-bone pendants,
each 1⅝″ long, ¼″ wide.

FIG. 138. NAVAJO BRACELET, 1930S.
Two stamped triangular silver wires with ends joined
in stamped discs; overlaid on each side is a row of
silver beading and an appliqué plate with an unusual
floral design. One very large turquoise set in a plain
bezel; surrounded by twisted and crimped silver wire
and silver beads.

FIG. 139. NAVAJO/PUEBLO NECKLACES, CORAL AND SILVER, 1920S–1930S.
Three strands of round coral beads are interspersed
with small globular and disc-shaped silver beads.

Fig. 140. Santa Clara Blackware Storage Jar, ca. 1930.
This is a fine example of the work done by Margaret
Tafoya. It is extremely large, evenly polished, and
evenly fired. Such high polished wares have become
popular in the expanding marketplace since the 1920s.

FIG. 141. ZIA POLYCHROME STORAGE JAR, CA. 1935.
Made by Trinidad Medina, this jar is unusually large
and exhibits design motifs commonly associated with
the best of Zia pottery. The birds and feather motifs
are trade marks of Medina's work.

FIG. 142. NAVAJO BRACELET, 1930s.
This cast silver bracelet has an oval turquoise centered
on an appliqué shield in the form of a stamped
"butterfly."

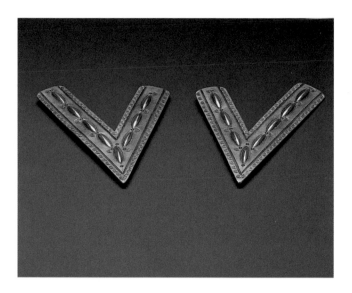

FIG. 143. NAVAJO COLLAR ORNAMENTS, 1930s.
Pair of silver collar ornaments: angled, flat, stamped.

FIG. 144. TAOS MICACEOUS PLAINWARE OPEN JAR, 1900–1930.
The base of this widely traded cooking ware piece was
molded in a basket and retains its markings. The body
has added coil decoration, common in Taos, Picuris,
and Plains Apache pottery. The micaceous clay needs
no additional temper and is highly serviceable.

FIG. 145. WESTERN APACHE BURDEN BASKET, 1930.
A classic basket, woven with plain twining with two
U-shaped reinforcing rods and a double rim. The
decorated bands are painted or stitched with
devil's claw.

FIG. 146. JICARILLA APACHE TRAY, 1930–1940.
An exceptionally fine basket, coiled with three-rod
foundation and decorated with an old design shared
with the Navajos and Pueblos.

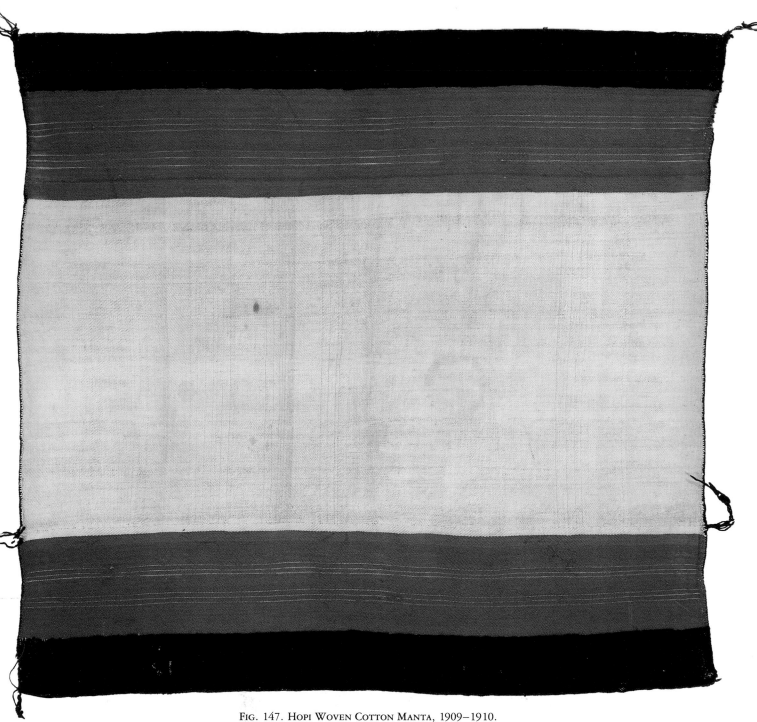

FIG. 147. HOPI WOVEN COTTON MANTA, 1909–1910.
Often called "maiden shawl," this type of manta was,
in fact, worn by women of all ages. It remains an
article of costume in many Pueblo ceremonies.

FIG. 150. HOPI SECOND MESA BASKET, CA 1930.

FIG. 148. COCHITI POLYCHROME JAR, CA. 1930.
This jar is unusual with its spectacular narrative painting. It depicts a buffalo hunt, with fanciful birds, mountain lions of Spanish style, and hunters chasing the animals.

FIG. 149. NAVAJO BASKET, 1900–1940.

FIG. 151. SAN CARLOS APACHE WATER BOTTLE, CA. 1930.

180

FIG. 152. HOPI MAN'S WEARING BLANKET, CA. 1930.
Black or brown and white wool-plaid patterned blankets were
traditional wear for Hopi men and boys until about 1880, when
other kinds of blankets were adopted, although plaid pieces like
this one were woven after 1880.

FIG. 153, 154. HOPI SECOND MESA BASKET AND LID, CA. MID-20TH CENTURY.

FIG. 155. SAN ILDEFONSO BLACK-ON-BLACK STORAGE JAR, CA. 1942.
This jar was signed by Maria and Julian Martinez. It is an
exceptionally large jar that, according to Margaret Tafoya, was made
by her mother Serafina for Maria and Julian. The practice of using
another potter's "greenware" to finish in a different style was a not
an uncommon method of production used to meet market demands.
The painting by Julian is exquisitely balanced in two bands, over a
fine polish, probably done by Maria's sister Clara Montoya.

FIG. 157. ZUNI SILVER RING WITH TURQUOISE AND JET MOSAIC, 1930s–1940s.

FIG. 156. PUEBLO/NAVAJO TOBACCO HORNS, 1920–1940.
The rounded end of each horn is decorated with
turquoise and jet mosaic. The horn on the left is
bisected by a single row of cream colored bone
squares. The opposite end of each contains a stopper
dyed dark purple.

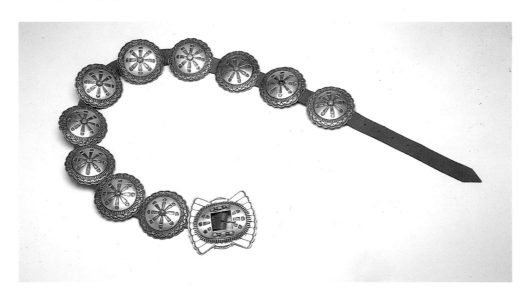

FIG. 158. COCHITI SILVER AND TURQUOISE CONCHA BELT, 1951.
This concha belt by Stanley Suina features round
conchas of silver overlay, each with one central
turquoise set, and a butterfly-shaped overlaid buckle
with turquoise sets. Made in 1951, it won first prize
at the Gallup Ceremonial and the Albuquerque
State Fair.

FIG. 159. JICARILLA APACHE BRACELET, 1951.
Copper overlay on silver, made by prizewinning smith
Abel Natsinneh.

FIG. 160. NAVAJO CONCHA BELT, 1948.
Innovative design by famed smith Kenneth Begay
utilizing linked spiral-shaped silver plaques, cut from
sheet metal.

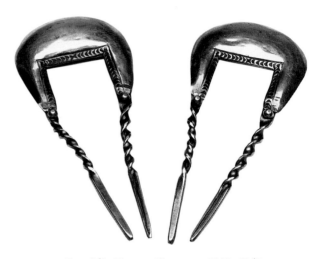

FIG. 161. NAVAJO KETOH, 1920s–1930s.
Wrought silver wrist guard with stamped and
repoussé decoration, on a leather band with incised
bull's head and outlined borders.

FIG. 162. NAVAJO HAIRPINS, 1900–1940.
Pair of silver hairpins: two twisted prongs soldered to
heads that are domed, filed, and decorated with
stamped designs and a pair of teardrops.

FIG. 163. HOPI BELT BUCKLE, 1954.
This buckle, set with turquoise and displaying the
Hopi-originated technique of silver overlay on silver,
was made by Hopi smith Louis Lomay (Lomatewa).

FIG. 164. SANTO DOMINGO BUCKLE, 1955.
Stamped silver overlay on copper, made by
Pasqualita Pacheco.

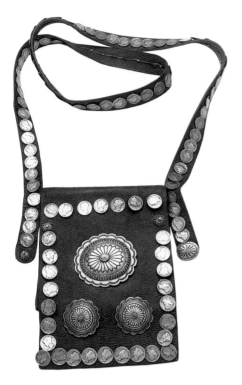

FIG. 165. NAVAJO SILVER DECORATED POUCH, CA. 1945.
Obtained at Santo Domingo Pueblo, this leather
pouch with shoulder strap is decorated with silver
liberty-head dimes; three stamped, fluted silver
buttons set with turquoise; and four stamped silver
conchas, three of which, set with turquoise, form the
central design.

FIG. 166. NAVAJO TWILL-WEAVE RUG OR
DOUBLE SADDLE BLANKET, CA. 1940.
In the latter half of the 19th century, Navajos wove
many twill-weave saddle blankets. The technique
produces a durable, closely woven fabric.

FIG. 167. HOPI THIRD MESA BASKET, 1920–1940.
This Hopi basket is plaited with sumac warps and
rabbit-brush wefts, chiefly natural dyes, and
traditional design motifs.

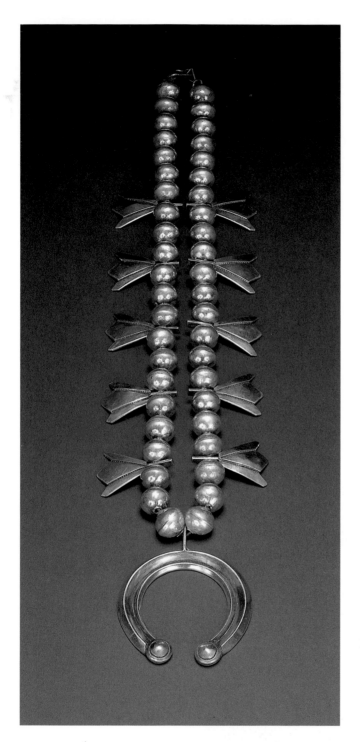

FIG. 169. SANTA CLARA POLYCHROME JAR, CA. 1940.
This is an example of the growing individualism of
potters who compete in the marketplace. The "Indian
Deco" style is an elaborate mixture of colored slips
with stylized morifs. The jar was made by Lela
Gutierrez and painted by her husband, Van.

FIG. 168. SANTO DOMINGO NECKLACE, 1955.
Innovative necklace by Reyes Chavez: a strand of
globular silver beads interspersed with stylized silver
blossoms that have been stamped and slightly domed.
The double *najahe* (which has irregular stamped
designs on the reverse) was cut from sheet metal,
stamped, then stamped bosses were soldered
to each end.

FIG. 170. WESTERN APACHE BURDEN BASKET, 1950.
This small basket has a double rim. The upper rod is
wood. The red bands are painted, the black is
devil's claw.

FIG. 171. HOPI PIKI TRAY, 1953.
Used to carry the rolls of paper-thin bread prepared for
ceremonial occasions, this tray is twill plaited with
splints of dune broom at the center and plaited around
the rim with rabbit brush. Made at Shungopovi by
Evelyn Peela.

FIG. 172. HOPI SECOND MESA BASKET, 1920.
The spread-winged eagle in this piece is a recurring
Hopi design motif. The colors are a mix of vegetal and
aniline dyes.

THE CONTEMPORARY PERIOD, POST-1960

Contemporary Southwest Indian craft arts continue to change and adapt to the demands of an ever growing commercial market. Today, many Indian communities rely on the sale of arts and crafts as one of their primary sources of cash income. Innovations and refinements continue, but usually in the context of a strong traditional inheritance.

FIG. 173. HOPI SECOND MESA BASKET, 1960.
This very tightly coiled piece features a Navajo
wedding basket design. Such baskets were used by the
Navajo in ceremonies regardless of whether they were
made by the Paiutes or the Hopi, and the Hopi
themselves carried them in dances and used them for a
variety of purposes.

FIG. 174. WESTERN APACHE WATER BOTTLE, 1900–1970.
This twined water bottle is worked in twill twine and
covered on both surfaces with piñon gum after having
been rubbed with red ocher. The rim is wrapped with
black devil's claw, which is also used to attach the
twig handles on the sides.

FIG. 175. ZUNI FETISH NECKLACE, 1984.
A type typical of the 1980s, this necklace consists of five strands of very
fine heishi, mixed near the ends with small tubular beads of turquoise
and coral interspersed with carved birds and animals of shell, turquoise,
and multicolored stones. Made by Lavina and Mary Tsikewa.

FIG. 176. NAVAJO/HOPI BRACELET AND RING SET, CA. 1960.
Bracelet: two stamped silver, heavy, triangular wires on each side
of a stamped, flat, sheet silver bar. A coiled rattlesnake of stamped
silver wire with punched eyes surrounds an oval flat turquoise set
in a plain bezel. Ring: three-prong, incised, split, silver band;
stamped silver rattlesnake with teardrop eyes and rattles; oval
turquoise set in a plain bezel.

FIG. 177. NAVAJO-SANTO DOMINGO NECKLACE, 1984.
Made by Gail Bird, Santo Domingo-Laguna, and
Yazzie Johnson, Navajo, this five-strand piece is
composed of beads of black onyx, white Chinese fossil,
and a single coral bead. Pendant and clasps are of
silver set with black Montana agate, with Mimbres bat
designs on the reverse.

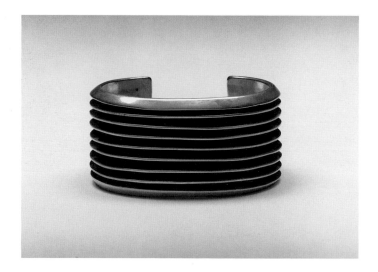

FIG. 178. ISLETA BRACELET, 1975.
This flanged silver bracelet has deeply
ridged plates set upright on an oxydized background,
a technique called "stacked silver" by the maker, Val
Jaramillo. The bracelet won first prize in category,
grand prize, and Bob Ward Indian Trader Award (ring
and earrings won second prize) at the Eight Northern
Indian Pueblos Artists and Craftsmen Show in 1975.

FIG. 179. NAVAJO SILVER NECKLACE, 1975.
Composed of one strand of graduated, semi-globular
fluted silver beads, this contemporary piece made by
Sarah Debois won first prize in its category at the
1975 Eight Northern Indian Pueblos Artists and
Craftsmen Show.

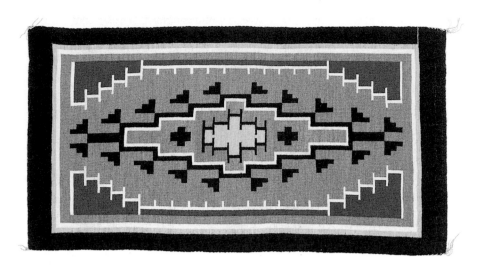

Fig. 180. Navajo Wall Hanging, Two Grey Hills, ca. 1970.

Fig. 181. Navajo Rug, Burntwater Style, 1981.
Woven by Philomena Yazzie, this rug exemplifies the
recent development in Navajo weaving in which pastel
vegetal dyes are combined with intricate designs
resembling those of contemporary Two Gray Hills,
Klageto, and some Ganado rugs.

FIG. 182. SANTA CLARA BLACKWARE "MELON" BOWL, 1981.
This "melon" bowl was made by noted potter Helen
Shupla. The forming of the jar was done when the clay
was wet by pushing out the ribs to create the "melon"
appearance.

FIG. 183. SANTA CLARA REDWARE "WEDDING" JAR, 1955
SAN ILDEFONSO BUFF-ON-SIENNA JAR, 1962
The deep carving on the wedding vase is a recent innovation (ca. 1924–1926) in
this traditional Santa Clara form, and was introduced by Serafina Tafoya. This
example was made by Teresita Naranjo. The jar at right was fired black, then
reoxidized to sienna. The Mimbres-inspired feathers were an innovation of Julian
Martinez. This piece was made by Maria and her son Popovi Da Martinez.

GLOSSARY

aniline a synthetic organic dye.

annealing a process by which silver is tempered to relieve internal stresses, first heated then rapidly cooled by plunging into water.

apocynum dog bane or Indian hemp. It was used in the prehistoric Southwest to obtain bast fibers from which to twist cordage.

appliqué a decorative element fastened to a larger surface.

awanyu Tewa name for the southwestern plumed or horned water serpent.

bas-relief carving in low relief so that the design is slightly raised above its background.

bentonite an absorptive clay mineral.

bevel to cut at a slant.

bezel a thin strip of metal rimming a stone and fastening it to its backing.

bezoar a hardened mass of hair from the stomach of a deer.

bivalve an invertebrate with an outer shell composed of two corresponding movable halves (e.g., clam).

braiding obliquely interweaving three or more elements which pass over and under their neighbors in a regular diagonal pattern.

breechclout a loincloth.

bridle horsegear consisting of headstall, bit, and reins.

bruised heart *see* Indented Heart.

bundle in basketry, a type of foundation usually consisting of grass, small stems, or splints.

burden basket a basket used to gather and carry food, firewood, or other items. It has a large open mouth and tapers toward the base. It is carried on the bearer's back with a strap across the forehead or shoulders.

burnish to achieve a lustre on pottery by rubbing the wet clay surface with a hard implement such as a polishing stone.

cabochon in gem cutting, a style in which the flat-based stone displays a high, domed, unfaceted apex.

carbon paint a vegetal pigment made from the residue of boiled stems and leaves of plants such as the Rocky Mountain Bee Plant. It sinks into the vessel's surface and fires a soft black. *See also* Guaco.

carding a combing process that aligns wool or cotton fibers before they are spun.

carinated keeled; ridged.

channel work inlaying a setting of multiple stones, each of which is separated by thin metal strips.

chee hands or "grandfather hands": small hand-shaped elements that appear as terminals on such Navajo articles as *najahes* and bracelets. Also known as "hands of Fatima," reflecting their presumed Near-Eastern origin.

chief blanket Navajo man's shoulder blanket with a distinctive pattern. Evolving from the simple striped shoulder blanket, it organized dark horizontal stripes into a solid broad band in the center of the blanket and in bands half again as wide along the top and bottom borders, with narrow, alternating white and black stripes on the ground between. Still later blue and red stripes were incorporated into these bands, and finally, increasingly complex figures were added within and at the edges of the bands.

chinking stones stones used to fill cracks or gaps.

churro wool obtained from the breed of Spanish sheep originally imported into the Southwest from Mexico. The sheep were well adapted to the southwestern environment, with long, staple wool that contained very little grease and was easily spun and dyed.

clay a finely textured mineral substance that is pliable when wet and can be hardened by firing. In addition to being modeled to form the vessel itself, diluted clay is used to make slip. *See also* Slip.

cluster style a group of stones set in individual bezels, somewhat larger than in row work or petit-point.

cochineal a red dye made from the dried bodies of female cochineal insects, which feed on the prickly pear cactus of Mexico and Central America.

cochiti slip a fine clay that is applied with a rag or a piece of soft leather and then rubbed with a cloth or with the palm of the hand.

coiling in pottery, the building up of vessel walls with ropes of clay laid one upon the other and pinched together. Also, the formation of basketry with a foundation consisting of rods and/or bundles of vegetal materials, laid next to one another and stitched together in spiral fashion.

cold chisel a steel tool with a short, straight cutting edge.

concha the Spanish word for shell applied, because of its appearance, to a metal plate, usually oval or round, with a radiating central pattern and scalloped edges.

concretion a mineral mass deposited inside a rock of a different composition.

conus a gastropod with a cone-shaped shell; *Conidae* family.

corrugated pottery textured ware in which the construction coils have been left partially exposed on some or all of the vessel's surface, creating an undulating or corrugated effect. These corrugations may be further manipulated with the fingers to produce patterned indentations.

countersinking inserting an object so that its highest point is at or below the surface of the setting into which it is placed.

crackling also called *crazing*. Fine cracks that appear in the slip after firing. Caused by a difference in the ratio of expansion and contraction between the slip and the body of the vessel.

crocheting a form of knitting (looping) accomplished with the aid of a hooked needle.

die in southwestern jewelry making, a metal stamp. A positive die is formed by cutting away portions of the surface of a scrap of steel to form a whole raised design. It is used to impress the design into an object to be decorated or to make a negative die by pressing the heated steel into a blank metal cylinder.

disc bead a centrally perforated bead with a diameter greater than its height.

domed overlay one of the Navajo jewelry making techniques that grew out of simple overlay in the mid–1970s. The upper layer of metal with cut-out design, positioned above a flat, oxidized background, takes the form of an arched dome.

ear tablet a flat sheet-like ear pendant.

effigy an image of a person, animal, or object.

embossing relief decoration of a flat surface in which a stamp, generally oval, is used to hammer a design into the metal from the reverse.

embroidery decoration applied to a fabric after weaving, employing a threaded needle.

etched shell a process developed by the Hohokam. It is thought to have been accomplished in the following manner: the surface of the shell was covered with gum or pitch, leaving portions exposed. When soaked in a weak solution of acetic acid, the exposed portion was eaten away and an engraved design remained.

fiber a slender filament which can be vegetal (e.g., grass, cotton) or animal (e.g., wool).

filing one of the earliest techniques used by Navajo smiths to decorate silver. Designs were cut into the metal using the edge of a file. (Somewhat later, the face of a file was impressed into a stamp blank to make an "end-of-a-file" design.)

fire cloud a blackened area on the surface of a vessel resulting when the fuel has rested on the spot during firing.

firing hardening a clay vessel by the application of heat. Traditional southwestern Indian pottery is not fired in a kiln but in the open, with fuel piled all around and burned.

firing atmosphere a term used in connection with the amount of air permitted to reach a vessel at various stages during firing. *See* Oxidizing Atmosphere; Oxygen Reducing Atmosphere.

floating in the manufacture of pottery, moistening to bring fine particles of clay to the vessel surface, which is then polished with a hard tool or worn stone. In weaving, a term which is applicable whenever a weft thread is passed unbound over two or more warp threads, or vice versa; this can occur on either surface of the fabric.

fluting a decorative treatment employing rounded grooves in the manner of pleating.

foundation in coiled basketry, the materials that are overlaid and held together by stitching.

fragment inlay a Navajo decorative technique developed around 1961 and today mostly produced on an assembly-line basis. It makes use of turquoise and coral chips inlaid mosaic-fashion into openings in the upper of two silver plates.

fret a pattern composed of small straight lines intersecting at right or oblique angles.

fugitive red a slip of red pigment applied after firing; this, unlike fired-on slips, is not permanent.

gastropod a univalve, or single shelled invertebrate (e.g., conch).

german silver a metal (an alloy of copper, zinc, and nickel) used in jewelry, particularly that of Plains tribes during the nineteenth century.

glaze a finely powdered mineral substance that melts during firing to form a glassy residue. Puebloans used glaze only to paint the design, not to coat the entire vessel.

glycymeris a marine bivalve: a bittersweet clam of the *Glycymeridae* family.

gorget a large ornament worn over the chest.

graving carving or shaping with a tool. In early Navajo silverwork, the term is often used to describe scratching a design into the surface with a file.

guaco a carbon paint made from the boiled residue of the Rocky Mountain Bee Plant.

half-twist in twined baskets, some of the strands may be twisted so that their darker bark surfaces face toward the exterior and form a pattern.

hands of fatima *See* Chee Hands.

hatching decoration consisting of closely spaced parallel lines.

headstall the part of a horse bridle that encircles the head. Navajo smiths—drawing upon Plains Indian and/or Mexican counterparts—began very early to make silver ornaments to decorate the leather straps forming the headstall.

heart-line a motif consisting of the figure of an animal, usually a deer, in which the heart is depicted with a line running between heart and mouth.

heddle a device used to facilitate laying in the weft by separating warp threads into sheds. In southwestern Indian weaving, the heddle consists of a continuous series of string loops attaching selected sets of warp threads to a shed stick. When the heddle is pulled, the warps attached to it are brought forward or up, depending upon the type of loom.

heishi small shell disc beads.

hematite red ochre: an earth iron ore widely used by southwestern Indians to make red paint.

herringbone a pattern made up of rows of parallel zigzag lines. In loom weaving and in basket weaving, a variety of twill.

hopi overlay a technique developed by Hopi smiths in the late 1930s in which a metal sheet with cut-out designs is soldered over a backing sheet; the cut-out areas are blackened by oxidation to provide greater contrast. (This technique is used by other groups.)

incising decoration applied by cutting into a surface, e.g., clay or metal, with a sharp tool.

incrustation covering with a hard coating. *See* overlay.

indented heart   a term used to describe the heart-shaped terminal of some crosses hung from southwestern silver bead necklaces. Also known as Bruised Heart or Lazy Heart.

indigo   a blue vegetal dye introduced into the Southwest by the Spaniards. It was purchased by Pueblos and Navajos to dye handspun yarn.

indurated   hardened.

ingot   metal cast in a trough mold for storing and later use.

inlay   to set stones or other substances in depressions carved into the surface being decorated.

jet   a mineral similar to coal which can be polished to a glossy black.

jokla   a short loop of disc beads, usually turquoise, set off with shell, originally worn strung through pierced ears and later hung from the bottom of stone and shell necklaces. Also known as *jaclaw*.

kachina   Puebloan supernatural being or carved figure representing said being.

ketoh   Navajo name for a wrist guard, worn to protect the archer's wrist from the snap of the bowstring. Prehistoric bowguards were fortified with hard substances such as shell or stone. In historic times, Navajos began to decorate the leather guard with silver plates.

"killed" pottery   a vessel in which a hole has been punched or drilled. It is thought that this was done so that its spirit might accompany that of the person with whom it was buried.

kiln   an oven used to fire pottery, capable of producing high, controlled heat.

kilt   among southwestern Indians, a man's short wrap-around skirt, today worn only on ceremonial occasions.

knitting   a process whereby a continuous strand of thread is interlaced in loops by means of needles.

labret   an ornament worn through a perforation in the lip.

labyrinth   in southwestern basket bowls, an allover pattern of continuous fret design.

lac   a resinous substance secreted by a scale insect that feeds on a host plant. Used in the manufacture of jewelry by the Hohokam, and in production of a red dye in the Near East and southern Asia, this dye appears in raveled yarns used in the Southwest, usually in specimens dating before 1860.

lapidary   having to do with the working of precious stones.

lazy heart   *See* Indented Heart.

lignite   a form of coal, especially one in which the original texture of the wood can be seen.

loom   a frame which supports warp threads, strung in a figure-eight configuration, through which weft threads are woven. The term "true loom" implies the use of heddles. Southwestern Indians developed a true loom in prehistoric times which continues in use today. Indian looms may be 1)*vertical* or *upright*: the bars over which warp threads are strung are attached to fixed bars that in turn are attached to a support above and an anchor below (the weaver sits on the ground in front and works upward); 2) *horizontal*: warp bars are positioned horizontally between four pegs driven into the ground (the weaver starts at one end and works toward the center as far as possible, and then moves to the opposite end, or weaves to the center and then sits on the finished portion and continues to the other end; 3) *backstrap* (used for narrow fabrics), also called *waist loom* or *belt loom*: consists of two sticks about 1½–2½ feet long between which warps are stretched; one end is fastened to a strap about the weaver's waist, the other to a tree, wall, or other nearby object (the weaver begins work at the waist bar and winds the finished cloth around it as necessary to keep the unfilled warps within easy reach). The Spaniards make use of a fourth type: a treadle or foot-operated loom on a horizontal frame.

looping   a single element weave in which a fabric is formed by a continuous series of interlocking coils.

lug   a projection, used as a handle.

majolica   a Spanish earthenware made of mixed clays with a lead-tin glaze, derived from the ancient Islamic East, which also came to be manufactured in the New World early in the sixteenth century. Mexican majolica was first brought into

the Southwest by Spaniards near the end of that century.

manta   a woven garment worn by Pueblos and Navajos either as a shoulder robe or as a dress. Pueblo women wear it as a shawl, or as a dress which is wrapped around the body and fastened at the right shoulder. Navajo women at first wove a similar manta, but soon devised a dress that was woven in two pieces and fastened at both shoulders; one type of Navajo shoulder blanket, displaying the typical Navajo dress pattern, is called "fancy manta."

manta pin   a long, sharpened silver pin with an ornamental head, used to hold the Navajo manta together.

matte   in pottery manufacture, a paint that fires to a dull, lusterless finish.

meander   a winding pattern.

mineral paint   pigment made from a mineral substance, such as iron oxide, mixed with water. Sometimes it may also be mixed with a vegetal binder. It produces a deep black, brownish-black, or reddish color, depending on the firing.

"moqui pattern"   a shoulder blanket pattern consisting of narrow stripes of indigo blue, brown, and white. It was called "Moqui" (an old term for Hopi) by nineteenth-century traders who erroneously attributed such textiles to the Hopis, although they were probably introduced from Mexico in the 1600s and were woven by Pueblos, Navajos, and Spaniards throughout the early historic period.

mosaic   in southwestern jewelry, a type of overlay or inlay ornamentation formed by cutting materials such as stone and/or shell into small pieces, shaping them to fit precisely together, and setting them side by side.

najahe (naja)   Navajo "crescent": a type of crescent-shaped pendant used to decorate horse bridles and later hung at the base of silver bead necklaces. It was introduced from Spain and originally from the Near East.

needlepoint   a Zuni style of decoration in which small, slender stones, pointed at both ends, are set into individual bezels in geometric patterns.

negative design   a secondary design created when a solid color covers all of a space except for selected areas of the lighter background.

nose plug   a plug-shaped ornament worn in a perforation in the nasal membrane.

olivella   a dwarf olive (a gastropod) with an elongated oval shell having a long narrow aperture. *Olividae* family.

olla   Spanish, *jar*. Used to describe Pueblo pottery jars made to contain food or water.

oxidizing atmosphere (oxidation firing). the result of a clean, smokeless fire which allows oxygen to circulate around the vessels being manufactured. It produces red, brown, tan, cream, and yellow colors.

oxygen reducing atmosphere (reduction firing)   an atmosphere in which air is not allowed to circulate freely around the vessels being fired. Used following oxidation, it produces white and gray pottery. A reducing atmosphere in which the fire is smothered with powdered manure near the end of the process is used to create a smoke whose carbon turns the pottery black.

overlay   to lay one material on top of another; i.e., in jewelry making, to lay a substance such as stone onto a backing such as bone, shell, leather, or stone. *See also* Hopi Overlay, Domed Overlay, Pedestal Overlay, Shadowbox.

overstitching   a form of ornamentation sometimes applied to Hopi coiled baskets in which a decorative, light colored stitch is placed over several darker coiling stitches, often at oblique or right angles to them, in order to emphasize or to add features to the design.

palette   a container for pigment.

peach basket   a small variety of Hopi burden basket.

pedestal overlay   cut-out figures mounted on pedestals upon slightly concave oxidized and stippled backgrounds.

pendleton blanket   machine-made blankets from the Pendleton Woolen Mills.

petit-point   in southwestern jewelry, a general term used to describe small stones set in individual bezels in geometric patterns. Needlepoint is a specific shape. Others, simply called petit-point, include round, oval, triangular, and teardrop.

pipe stamp   the end of a pipe was sometimes used by early Navajo smiths to stamp circles on articles of silver. When cut in half lengthwise, a crescent-shaped stamp was created.

plaid   a checker weave. When used to fashion a Hopi man's shoulder blanket, its patterns are woven in black and white, visible in both warp and twill weft.

plaiting   in basket weaving, single elements or sets of elements, either flexible or rigid, are passed over and under one another. Patterns are created by alternating the sequence of the weave or by using different colored materials.

ply   a single strand of yarn or thread. In single-ply yarn, fibers have been twisted into one continuous thread in one spinning. Two or more single plies may be twisted together to yield two-, three-, four-, or multiple-ply yarns.

polishing stone   a small worn stone used to rub the surface of a vessel while still damp, in order to obtain a smooth, lustrous finish. Polishing stones are often heirlooms passed from mother to daughter.

polychrome   decoration using three or more colors in the overall pattern.

poncho   a type of serape with a slit in the center for the head, fashioned after the Mexican variety.

positive die   *See* Die.

potsherd   a fragment of broken pottery.

puki   a base or turning device: usually a bowl-shaped clay container in which the modeled base of a vessel is formed; it is also used to rotate the vessel while building up its walls.

pump drill   a device whereby a drill shaft is rotated by raising and lowering a bow or bar with a cord at its center that is attached to the upper end of the shaft.

rag-wiped   a term used in reference to pottery that has been polished with a piece of fabric rather than a polishing stone.

"rain bird" design   a pottery motif consisting of a stylized bird form: primarily a coil or scroll to which other elements may be appended.

raveled yarn   yarn acquired by raveling each individual thread from a piece of woolen trade fabric. Before easy-to-use aniline dyes became readily available, Navajos and Pueblos used this method of obtaining a rich red color that could not be procured with native dyes. Lac- and cochineal-dyed imported cloth, often called by the Spanish term "bayeta" (English, "baize"), was first employed for the purpose. After about 1870 it was replaced by aniline-dyed American trade flannel. Raveled yarns were used in blanket weaving by the Navajos, but Pueblos used them mostly as embroidery thread.

reducing atmosphere   *See* Oxygen Reducing Atmosphere.

repoussage   relief decoration of a flat surface by hammering a pattern from the reverse. Usually emphasized by stamping on the front, around the edges of the image.

resist-dye   in weaving, portions of the fabric are protected from the dye bath, forming a pattern.

ring basket   a sturdy, plaited, bowl-shaped body tied over a ring-shaped rod which forms the rim. Used to winnow wheat and wash grains.

rocker engraving   an early form of decoration on metal using a small tool with a chisel-like edge; this was pushed forward while at the same time rocking it from side to side in order to form a zig-zag pattern. Ceased to be used around 1875.

rod   in basket making, a single, straight, slender wooden stick.

row work   a Zuni style of decoration consisting of small stones, usually turquoises, in individual bezels, arranged in closely set rows.

saltillo-style   a style of decoration characteristic of blankets woven in Saltillo, Mexico. Typical features include a large central serrate diamond and rows of tiny figures.

schist   a metamorphic crystalline rock that may be split along parallel planes.

scoring   marking with lines or grooves.

scroll   a spiral-shaped form.

serape   a type of man's shoulder blanket, derived from Mexico, woven longer than wide.

serrate toothed or sharply notched.

sgraffito scratching through the slip to uncover the color of the clay beneath.

shadowbox developed around the mid-1950s, this is a type of silver overlay in which the upper plate is arched above a "box" of inner walls containing appliqué decoration on an oxidized background.

shed in a loom, the triangular space through which weft is passed, formed by manipulating groups of warp threads, pulling some forward and some to the rear.

slat in basketry, a thin, narrow, flat strip of wood.

slip a very fine clay watered down to a cream-like consistency. It is used to change the color and/or texture of the pot's surface in order to form a suitable background on which to paint the design.

smudging the intentional smoke-blackening of a vessel surface.

solder a metal alloy used when melted to join metallic surfaces.

spider woman cross on Navajo baskets, a design motif consisting of a red equilateral cross outlined in black.

spin-casting (machine-casting; lost-wax casting) a rubber mold is made of a hand-made ornament, from which wax duplicates can then be fabricated. These are connected by ducts, surrounded by plaster, then heated in a metal container to melt away the wax, leaving hollow plaster molds. Finally, the container is spun on a motor-driven arm, pumping molten silver from an attached container into the cavities by centrifugal force. The finished products are often very difficult to distinguish from the original article.

spindle a device for twisting fibers together into one continuous strand. Southwestern Indian spindles consist of a slender pointed stick, or shaft, and a whorl, or weight, or a smaller stick fastened to the shaft between the center and one of its ends.

splint a very slender, flexible twig or strip of wood.

stablized turquoise turquoise of a soft grade that has been hardened by filling the pores with plastic resins and chemicals; this process also darkens and enhances the color.

squash blossom Navajo silversmiths make these pendants by attaching a conical "blossom" to a spherical bead. This form is thought to have derived from a Mexican trouser button called a "pomegranate blossom."

"stacked" silver also called "flanged" silver, it is a decorative technique that features thin silver plates set on edge, side by side.

stamp in jewelry making, a tool with a relief design at the end; it is used to impress the design into metal. *See also* Die; Pipe Stamp.

stepped lines terraced lines that resemble stair steps.

stippled decorated with small short lines or dots.

stirrup vessel one with a handle connecting two spouts.

stitching joining by an in-and-out lacing of threads.

stitch-and-wrap coiling a coiling technique in which the sewing weft is brought around the coil, then wrapped around itself to make a kind of knot, also creating a space between stitches.

"storyteller" a ceramic figurine composed of an adult (originally "grandfather") to which are attached any number of tiny children. Developed by Cochiti potter Helen Cordero in the mid-1960s from an earlier tradition of Pueblo—especially Cochiti—clay figurines, this style became immensely popular and is now produced by many groups and features not only human but sometimes animal protagonists.

tablita tablet-shaped ceremonial headdress worn by Pueblo dancers.

tapestry weave a plain weft-face weave in which weft threads are tightly compressed, completely hiding the warp.

teardrop in silver work, a small globule used as an appliqué ornament. Also called "raindrop."

temper a coarse material mixed with clay in order to promote even drying and workability, prevent cracking, and provide for safer firing. Some of the most common tempers include sand, pulverized rocks, and ground potsherds.

three-strand twining in basket making, a twine weave in which three weft elements are twisted; each one, as it passes inward, is carried behind the warp stem adjoining so that, in a whole revolution, the three weft elements have in turn passed behind three warp elements.

ticked decorated with a series of small, parallel markings.

tinklers dangles of tin or bone or stone which make a jingling sound when struck together.

three-ring dating the use of certain types of wooden beams (especially pine, fir, piñon) to determine age and therefore the age of associated artifacts. Each year a tree adds a growth ring—wider or narrower depending upon the amount of moisture available that year. This produces a pattern which is constant over a wide geographic area. A master tree-ring calendar, built up using overlapping samples, has been created for use in dating archaeological sites. Also known as *dendrochronology*.

tufa a porous, stream-deposited rock.

tuff rock composed of fine volcanic detritus.

tumpline a carrying band, 10–12" long, with a loop at each end, worn over the forehead. Ropes are strung through the loops to support a load carried on the back.

twill weave a weave in which the weft element is carried over one and under two or more warp elements and, as weaving progresses, each series is moved one element to the right or left of the series below, producing diagonal lines or ribs on the surface of the fabric/basket. Variations include 1) *diagonal twill*: the weaving progresses without interruption from one side of the article to the other; 2) *herringbone twill*: the weaving proceeds in opposite directions from a common center, creating horizontal zigzags; 3) *diamond twill*: horizontal zigzags are reversed in the following row, creating a diamond pattern.

twill plaiting   a term for a basketry technique. *See* Twill Weave.

twill twining   a basket weave in which two weft elements are twined around the warps in a diagonal twill pattern. *See also* Twining.

twining   in basketry, this technique involves twisting two or more horizontal elements (wefts) around each other as they are woven in and out of more rigid vertical elements (warps). Also a finger weave termed "twined weft."

two-faced weave   a distinctive weave sometimes employed by Navajos. On the upright loom four heddles are required, two throwing long weft floats to the foreground of the textile and two throwing long weft floats to the back. This allows one pattern to be built up on the front (facing the weaver), and an entirely different pattern on the reverse (usually simple stripes).

type   a classification given to a group of pottery vessels with similar characteristics.

umbo   a protrusion occurring just above the hinge on each half of a bivalve shell.

ware   a group of related pottery types sharing similar technological features.

warp   parallel elements that run longitudinally, crossed by and interwoven with transverse elements.

wedding basket design   a traditional design, often seen on Navajo basket bowls, in which a red band is bordered on both sides by black triangles; the entire pattern is split at one point to form a pathway from base to rim.

wedding vase   a type of pottery vessel having two spouts connected by a handle. *See* Stirrup Vessel.

wedge weave   a process by which weft stripes are beaten into the warps at an angle. In the next band of stripes, the angle is reversed, resulting in a pulling of the warps in opposite directions and a scalloped effect along the edges of the fabric.

weft   transverse elements which cross and interwork with the warp elements.

weft-wrap openwork   a technique used to create openwork designs on plain weave cloth; small holes are made during weaving by drawing apart certain warps and wefts and wrapping them with selected weft threads.

welt   a thin strip of tough fiber sometimes inserted into a foundation with one or two rods to strengthen the coil and fill the space between the rods.

whirlwind design   a curvilinear element with spiral arms.

wicker   a basket weave in which a rigid warp and a slender flexible weft are interwoven, creating the surface effect of a series of ridges.

wire   some of the earliest southwestern bracelets were made from brass and copper wire obtained by trade. Navajo smiths later produced their own silver wire. Round, square, and carinated were the most common shapes. By the early 1900s, wire of these kinds could be obtained commercially, as could bead wire, imitating a row of teardrops. A single wire could be used alone, or two or more might be combined, as in a popular style originating in the 1920s in which two round wires were twisted together. Crimped wire is bezel wire bent into a zigzag pattern and used—like bead wire—as a decorative appliqué.

withe   a slender pliable branch or stick.

yarn   a general term for an assemblage of fibers spun together into a continuous strand.

yei   Navajo supernatural being.

Suggested Reading

The Southwest: An Overview

CORDELL, LINDA S. *Prehistory of the Southwest*. Orlando: Academic Press, 1984.

JENNINGS, JESSE D. *Prehistory of North America*. New York: McGraw-Hill, 1968.

MARTIN, PAUL S., AND FRED PLOG. *The Archaeology of Arizona*. New York: Doubleday, 1973.

ORTIZ, ALFONSO, ED. *Southwest*. Vols. 9 and 10, Handbook of North American Indians. Washington, D.C.: Smithsonian Institution, 1979.

SPICER, EDWARD H. *Cycles of Conquest: The Impact of Spain, Mexico and the United States on the Indians of the Southwest, 1533– 1960*. Tucson: University of Arizona Press, 1962.

Southwestern Baskets

ALLEN, LAURA GRAVES, ROBERT BREUNIG, ET AL. "The Basket Weavers: Artisans of the Southwest." *Plateau* 53:4. Museum of Northern Arizona, Flagstaff.

BREAZEALE, J. F. *The Pima and His Basket*. Tucson: Arizona Archaeological and Historical Society, 1932.

CAÍN, H. THOMAS. *Pima Indian Basketry*. Heard Museum Research Project no. 2. Phoenix: Heard Museum of Anthropology and Primitive Art, 1962.

DEWALD, TERRY. *The Papago Indians and Their Basketry*. Tucson: Terry DeWald, 1979.

ELLIS, FLORENCE H., AND MARY WALPOLE. "Possible Pueblo, Navajo, and Jicarilla Basketry Relationships." *El Palacio* 66: 181–198.

FERG, ALLAN, AND WILLIAM B. KESSEL. *Western Apache Material Culture*. Tucson: University of Arizona Press, 1987.

GOGOL, JOHN M. "Pima Indian Basketry." *American Indian Basketry Magazine* 2:3 (1982) and 3:3 (1983).

HAURY, EMIL W. *Painted Cave, Northeastern Arizona*. Dragoon, Ariz.: Amerind Foundation, Inc., 1945.

HEROLD, JOYCE. "The Basketry of Tanzanita Pesata." *American Indian Art Magazine* 3:2 (1978).

———. "Havasupai Basketry: Theme and Variation." *American Indian Art Magazine* 4:4 (1979).

KISSELL, MARY LOIS. "Basketry of the Papago and Pima." In *Anthropological Papers of the American Museum of Natural History* 17:4, New York, 1916.

LAMBERT, MARJORIE F., AND RICHARD AMBLER. *A Survey and Excavation of Caves in Hidalgo County, New Mexico*. Santa Fe: School of American Research, 1965.

MASON, OTIS TUFTON. *Aboriginal American Basketry: Studies in a Textile Art without Machinery*. Annual Report of the Smithsonian Institution for 1902, Washington, D.C., 1904.

MAULDIN, BARBARA. *Traditions in Transition: Contemporary Basketry Weaving of the Southwestern Indians*. Santa Fe: Museum of New Mexico Press, 1984.

McGREEVY, SUSAN BROWN, AND ANDREW HUNTER WHITEFORD. *Translating Tradition: Basketry Arts of the San Juan Paiute*. Santa Fe: Wheelwright Museum of the American Indian, 1985.

McKEE, BARBARA AND EDWIN, AND JOYCE HEROLD. *Havasupai Baskets and Their Makers: 1930–1940*. Flagstaff: Northland Press, 1975.

MORRIS, EARL H., AND ROBERT F. BURGH. *Anasazi Basketry: Basket Maker II through Pueblo III*. Carnegie Institution of Washington, Publication 533. Washington, D.C., 1941.

ROBERTS, HELEN H. "Basketry of the San Carlos Apache." In *Anthropological Papers of the American Museum of Natural History* 21:2, New York, 1929.

ROBINSON, BERT. *The Basket Weavers of Arizona*. Albuquerque: University of New Mexico Press, 1954.

STEVENSON, JAMES. "Illustrated Catalogue of the Collections Obtained from the Pueblos of Zuni, New Mexico, and Wolpi, Arizona, in 1881." In *Third Annual Report of the Bureau of American Ethnology*. Washington, D.C.: Government Printing Office, 1884.

TANNER, CLARA LEE. *Apache Indian Baskets*. Tucson: University of Arizona Press, 1982.

———. *Indian Baskets of the Southwest*. Tucson: University of Arizona Press, 1983.

WELTFISH, GENE. "Problems in the Study of Ancient and Modern Basket-Makers." *American Anthropologist*, n.s., 34:108–117.

WHITEFORD, ANDREW HUNTER. *Southwestern Indian Baskets: Their History and Their Makers*. Santa Fe: School of American Research, 1988.

Prehistoric Pottery of New Mexico

BRODY, J. J. *Mimbres Painted Pottery*. (School of American Research.) Albuquerque: University of New Mexico Press, 1977.

DITTERT, ALFRED E., JR., AND FRED PLOG. *Generations in Clay: Pueblo Pottery of the American Southwest*. Flagstaff: Northland Press, 1980.

HARLOW, FRANCIS H. *Matte-Paint Pottery of the Tewa, Keres, and Zuni Pueblos*. Santa Fe: Museum of New Mexico Press, 1973.

LEBLANC, STEVEN A. *The Mimbres People: Ancient Pueblo Painters of the American Southwest*. New York: Thames and Hudson, 1983.

LISTER, ROBERT H., AND FLORENCE C. LISTER. *Anasazi Pottery: Ten Centuries of Prehistoric Ceramic Art in the Four Corners Country of the Southwestern United States*. Albuquerque: Maxwell Museum of Anthropology, University of New Mexico, 1978.

MERA, H. P. "Style Trends of Pueblo Pottery in the Rio Grande and Little Colorado Cultural Areas from the Sixteenth to the Nineteenth Century." *Memoirs of the Laboratory of Anthropology* 3. Santa Fe, 1939.

SHEPARD, ANNA O. *Ceramics for the Archaeologist*. Carnegie Institution of Washington Publication, 1956.

Historic and Contemporary Southwestern Pottery

ARNOLD, DAVID L. "Pueblo Pottery, 2000 Years of Artistry." *National Geographic Magazine* 162 (November 1982).

BATKIN, JONATHAN. *Pottery of the Pueblos of New Mexico, 1700–1940*. Colorado Springs: Taylor Museum, 1987.

BUNZEL, RUTH L. *The Pueblo Potter: A Study of Creative Imagination in Primitive Art*, 1929. New York: Dover Publications, 1972.

COE, RALPH T. *Lost and Found Traditions: Native American Art 1965–1985*. Seattle: University of Washington Press, in association with the American Federation of Arts, 1986.

DITTERT, ALFRED E., JR., AND FRED PLOG. *Generations in Clay: Pueblo Pottery of the American Southwest*. Flagstaff: Northland Press, in cooperation with the American Federation of the Arts, 1980.

FRANK, LARRY, AND FRANCIS HARLOW. *Historic Pottery of the Pueblo Indians, 1600–1880*. Boston: New York Graphic Society, 1974.

HARLOW, FRANCIS H. *Matte-Paint Pottery of the Tewa, Keres and Zuni Pueblos*. Santa Fe: Museum of New Mexico Press, 1973.

———. *Modern Pueblo Pottery, 1880–1960*. Flagstaff: Northland Press, 1977.

HEDGES, KEN, AND ALFRED E. DITTERT, JR. *Heritage in Clay*. In San Diego Museum Papers, no. 17. 1984.

LEFREE, BETTY. *Santa Clara Pottery Today*. Albuquerque: University of New Mexico Press, 1975. Published for the School of American Research.

MARIOTT, ALICE. *Maria: The Potter of San Ildefonso*. Norman, Okla.: University of Oklahoma Press, 1948.

MAXWELL MUSEUM OF ANTHROPOLOGY. *Seven Families in Pueblo Pottery*. Albuquerque: The University of New Mexico Press, 1974.

MERA, H. P. *Style Trends of Pueblo Pottery in the Rio Grande and Little Colorado Cultural Areas from the Sixteenth to the Nineteenth Century*. Memoirs of the Laboratory of Anthropology, vol. 3, Santa Fe, 1939.

———. *Pueblo Designs, 176 Illustrations of the "Rain Bird,"* 1937. New York: Dover Publications, 1970.

PETERSON, SUSAN. *Lucy M. Lewis, American Indian Potter*. Tokyo and New York: Kodansha International, 1984.

———. *The Living Tradition of Maria Martinez*. Tokyo and New York: Kodansha International, 1979.

SHEPARD, ANNA O. *Ceramics for the Archaeologist*, Publication 609, Carnegie Institution of Washington, Washington, D.C., 1965.

SMITH, WATSON, RICHARD B. WOODBURY, AND NATHALIE F. S. WOODBURY. "The Excavation of Hawikuh by Frederick Webb Hodge." In *Report of the Hendricks-Hodge Expedition*, 1917–1923. New York: Museum of the American Indian, Heye Foundation, 1966.

TOULOUSE, BETTY. *Pueblo Pottery of the New Mexico Indians*. Santa Fe: Museum of New Mexico Press, 1977.

WADE, EDWIN L., AND LEA S. MCCHESNEY. *Historic Hopi Ceramics*. The Thomas V. Keam Collection of the Peabody Museum of Archaeology and Ethnology. Cambridge: Peabody Museum Press, Harvard University, 1981.

———. *America's Great Lost Expedition: The Thomas Keam Collection of Hopi Pottery from the Second Hemenway Expedition, 1890–1894*. Phoenix: The Heard Museum, 1980.

WHEELWRIGHT MUSEUM OF THE AMERICAN INDIAN. *The Red and the Black, Santa Clara Pottery by Margaret Tafoya.* Santa Fe: Wheelwright Museum, 1983.

Southwestern Jewelry

ADAIR, JOHN. *The Navajo and Pueblo Silversmiths.* Norman: University of Oklahoma Press, 1944.

BEDINGER, MARGERY. *Indian Silver: Navajo and Pueblo Jewelers.* Albuquerque: University of New Mexico Press, 1973.

BRADFIELD, WESLEY. *Cameron Creek Village.* Monographs of the School of American Research, no. 1. Santa Fe, 1931.

EZELL, PAUL. "Shell Work of the Prehistoric Southwest." In *The Kiva* 3(1937).

FRANK, LARRY, AND MILLARD J. HOLBROOK II. *Indian Silver Jewelry of the Southwest: 1868–1930.* Boston: New York Graphic Society, 1978.

GLADWIN, HAROLD S.; EMIL W. HAURY; E. B. SAYLES; AND NORA GLADWIN. "Excavations at Snaketown: I Material Culture." Gila Pueblo, *Medallion Papers,* no. 25(1937).

HAURY, EMIL W. "Minute Beads from Prehistoric Pueblos." *American Anthropologist* 33(1931).

———. *The Stratigraphy and Archaeology of Ventana Cave.* Tucson: University of Arizona Press, and Albuquerque: University of New Mexico Press, 1950.

HEWETT, EDGAR L. *The Chaco Canyon and Its Monuments.* Albuquerque: University of New Mexico Press, 1936.

HODGE, FREDERICK WEBB. "Hawikuh Bonework." In *Indian Notes and Monographs,* vol. 3, no. 3. New York: Museum of the American Indian, Heye Foundation, 1920.

———. "Turquois [sic] Work of Hawikuh New Mexico," In *Leaflets of the Museum of the American Indian,* no. 2. Heye Foundation, 1921.

JERNIGAN, E. WESLEY. *Jewelry of the Prehistoric Southwest.* School of American Research Southwest Indian Art Series. Albuquerque: University of New Mexico Press, 1978.

KIDDER, ALFRED V. *The Artifacts of Pecos.* Robert S. Peabody Foundation for Archaeology. Andover: Phillips Academy, 1932.

KING, DALE STUART. *Indian Silverwork of the Southwest,* Vol. 2. Tucson: Dale Stuart King Publisher, 1976.

LUND, MARSHA MAYER. *Indian Jewelry, Fact and Fantasy.* Boulder: Paladin Press, 1979.

MARTIN, PAUL S., ET AL. Mogollon Cultural Continuity and Change. Fieldiana: Anthropology, vol. 40, Chicago.

MCGREGOR, JOHN C. "Burial of an Early American Magician." In *Proceedings of the American Philosophical Society,* 86(1943), Philadelphia.

MERA, H. P. *Indian Silverwork of the Southwest, Volume I.* Tucson: Dale Stuart King Publisher, 1959.

MATTHEWS, WASHINGTON. "Navajo Silversmiths." In Second Annual Report, U.S. Bureau of American Ethnology, Washington, D.C.

MORRIS, EARL H. "The Aztec Ruin." In *American Museum of Natural History Anthropological Papers,* vol. 26 (Part I), New York, 1919.

MORRIS, EARL H. AND R. F. BURGH, *Basket Maker II Sites Near Durango, Colorado.* Carnegie Institution of Washington, Publication 604, Washington, D.C.

MORRIS, ELIZABETH. "Basketmaker Caves in the Prayer Rock District, Northeastern Arizona." Ph.D. dissertation, University of Arizona, 1958.

MOTT, DOROTHY CHALLIS. "Progress of the Excavations at Kinishba." In *The Kiva* 2(1936).

PARRISH, LARAYNE. "The Stylistic Development of Navajo Jewelry." In *Southwest Indian Silver From the Doneghy Collection,* edited by Louise Lincoln. The Minneapolis Institute of Arts. Austin: University of Texas Press, 1982.

PEPPER, GEORGE H. "Pueblo Bonito." In *American Museum of Natural History Anthropological Papers,* vol. 27, New York, 1905.

STUBBS, STANLEY A., AND W. S. STALLINGS, JR. *The Excavation of Pindi Pueblo, New Mexico.* Monographs of the School of American Research and Laboratory of Anthropology, no. 18, Santa Fe.

WHEAT, JOE BEN. "Early Southwest Metalwork." In *Southwest Indian Silver From the Doneghy Collection,* edited by Louise Lincoln. The Minneapolis Institute of Arts. Austin: University of Texas Press, 1982.

WOODWARD, ARTHUR. *A Brief History of Navajo Silversmithing.* Flagstaff: Northland Press, 1971.

WRIGHT, MARGARET. *Hopi Silver.* Flagstaff: Northland Press, 1972.

Southwestern Textiles

AMSDEN, CHARLES AVERY. *Navajo Weaving, Its Technique and History,* 1934. The Fine Arts Press, Santa Ana, California, in cooperation with the Southwest Museum. Layton, UT.: Peregrine Smith, 1975.

DOUGLAS, FREDERIC H. *Pueblo Indian Clothing.* Denver Art Museum, Indian Leaflet Series, no. 4(1930).

————. *The Navajo Indians.* Denver Art Museum, Indian Leaflet Series, no. 21(1931).

DUTTON, BERTHA P. *Sun Father's Way: The Kiva Murals of Kuaua.* Albuquerque: University of New Mexico Press, 1963.

EL PALACIO EDITORS. *Navajo Weaving Handbook.* Santa Fe: Museum of New Mexico Press, 1977.

FOX, NANCY. *Pueblo Weaving and Textile Arts.* Santa Fe: Museum of New Mexico Press, 1978.

HIBBEN, FRANK C. *Kiva Art of the Anasazi at Pottery Mound.* Las Vegas, Nev.: K C Publications, 1975.

KENT, KATE PECK. "The Cultivation and Weaving of Cotton in the Prehistoric Southwestern United States." In *Transactions of the American Philosophical Society,* n.s., vol. 47, part 3, Philadelphia, 1957.

————. *Navajo Weaving.* Phoenix: The Heard Museum, 1961.

————. "Pueblo and Navajo Weaving Traditions and the Western World." In *Ethnic and Tourist Arts,* edited by Nelson H. H. Graburn, pp. 85–101. Berkeley: University of California Press, 1976.

————. "Pueblo Weaving." *American Indian Art Magazine,* 7 (1981): pp. 32–45.

————. *Textiles of the Prehistoric Southwest.* School of American Research Southwest Indian Arts Series. Albuquerque: University of New Mexico Press, 1983a.

————. *Pueblo Indian Textiles: A Living Tradition.* Santa Fe: School of American Research Press, 1983b.

————. *Navajo Weaving: Three Centuries of Change.* Santa Fe: School of American Research Press, 1985.

MERA, H. P. *Pueblo Indian Embroidery.* Laboratory of Anthropology Memoir no. 4, Santa Fe, 1943.

————. *Navajo Textile Arts.* Laboratory of Anthropology, Santa Fe, 1948. Layton, Ut: Peregrine Smith, 1975.

RODEE, MARIAN. *Southwestern Weaving.* Albuquerque: University of New Mexico Press, 1977.

————. *Old Navajo Rugs, Their Development from 1900 to 1940.* Albuquerque: University of New Mexico Press, 1981.

ROEDIGER, VIRGINIA MORE. *Ceremonial Costumes of the Pueblo Indians.* Berkeley: University of California Press, 1941.

SMITH, WATSON. *Kiva Mural Decorations at Awatovi and Kawaika-a.* In Papers of the Peabody Museum of Archaeology and Ethnology, vol. 38 (Reports of the Awatovi Expedition, no. 5), Harvard University, Cambridge, 1952.

WHEAT, JOE BEN. Spanish-American and Navajo Weaving, 1600 to Now. In *Collected Papers in Honor of Marjorie Ferguson Lambert,* edited by Albert H. Schroeder. Papers of the Archaeological Society of New Mexico, no. 3, pp. 199–226. Albuquerque Archaeological Society Press, 1976.

————. "Rio Grande, Pueblo, and Navajo Weavers: Cross-Cultural Influence." In *Spanish Textile Tradition of New Mexico and Colorado.* Santa Fe: Museum of International Folk Art, Museum of New Mexico Press, 1979.

INDEX